CW01337733

The ROBIN ALMANAC

In his own words

Helping robins to thrive all year round, and jobs not to be doing in the garden, month by month.

By A. ROBIN, Esq.

Illustrated by Robert Stephen Parry

To Mrs Robin

ISBN: 9798864749029

© *A. Robin, Esq. 2023.*

All rights reserved. Except for the quotation of short passages for commentary or review, no part of this publication may be reproduced, sung from tree-tops, stored in a retrieval system or transmitted in any form, electronic, mechanical or otherwise without the prior permission of the author and publisher.

en– gb used throughout

A. Robin, Esq. is also author of:
'The Magnificent British Garden Robin – *in his Own Words*'

CONTENTS

INTRODUCTION	1
JANUARY	9
WHAT ROBINS DO IN JANUARY	10
HELPING ROBINS THROUGH JANUARY	12
ROBIN'S PLANT OF THE MONTH – THE SNOWDROP	17
JOBS NOT TO BE DOING IN THE GARDEN DURING JANUARY	19
THE NIGHT SKY IN JANUARY	20
'PERHAPS' AND 'MAYBE' FOR ROBINS IN JANUARY	22
FEBRUARY	27
WHAT ROBINS DO IN FEBRUARY	29
HELPING ROBINS THROUGH FEBRUARY	33
ROBIN'S PLANT OF THE MONTH – THE DAFFODIL	35
JOBS NOT TO BE DOING IN THE GARDEN DURING FEBRUARY	36
THE NIGHT SKY IN FEBRUARY	37
'PERHAPS' AND 'MAYBE' FOR ROBINS IN FEBRUARY	38

MARCH — 43

- What Robins do in March — 45
- Helping Robins through March — 48
- Robin's plant of the month – the Primrose — 50
- Jobs not to be doing in the Garden during March — 51
- The Night Sky in March — 53
- 'Perhaps' and 'maybe' for Robins in March — 54

APRIL — 59

- What Robins do in April — 60
- Helping Robins through April — 62
- Robin's plants of the month – wild Garlic and English Bluebells — 66
- Jobs not to be doing in the Garden during April — 67
- The Night Sky in April — 69
- 'Perhaps' and 'maybe' for Robins in April — 71

MAY — 77

- What Robins do in May — 79
- Helping Robins through May — 83
- Robin's plant of the month – Hawthorn — 84
- Jobs not to be doing in the Garden during May — 86
- The Night Sky in May — 88
- 'Perhaps' and 'maybe' for Robins in May — 89

JUNE	**95**
WHAT ROBINS DO IN JUNE	97
HELPING ROBINS THROUGH JUNE	99
ROBIN'S PLANT OF THE MONTH – THE WILD ROSE	101
JOBS NOT TO BE DOING IN THE GARDEN DURING JUNE	102
THE NIGHT SKY IN JUNE	104
'PERHAPS' AND 'MAYBE' FOR ROBINS IN JUNE	106
JULY	**111**
WHAT ROBINS DO IN JULY	113
HELPING ROBINS THROUGH JULY	116
ROBIN'S PLANT OF THE MONTH – HONEYSUCKLE	117
JOBS NOT TO BE DOING IN THE GARDEN DURING JULY	118
THE NIGHT SKY IN JULY	120
'PERHAPS' AND 'MAYBE' FOR ROBINS IN JULY	121
AUGUST	**127**
WHAT ROBINS DO IN AUGUST	128
HELPING ROBINS THROUGH AUGUST	129
ROBIN'S PLANT OF THE MONTH – ENGLISH LAVENDER	130
JOBS NOT TO BE DOING IN THE GARDEN DURING AUGUST	132
THE NIGHT SKY IN AUGUST	137
'PERHAPS' AND 'MAYBE' FOR ROBINS IN AUGUST	138

SEPTEMBER — 143

- What Robins do in September — 144
- Helping Robins through September — 147
- Robin's plant of the month – Asters — 149
- Jobs not to be doing in the Garden during September — 151
- The Night Sky in September — 153
- 'Perhaps' and 'maybe' for Robins in September — 155

OCTOBER — 161

- What Robins do in October — 162
- Helping Robins through October — 164
- Robin's plant of the month – the Spindle Tree — 168
- Jobs not to be doing in the Garden during October — 169
- The Night Sky in October — 171
- 'Perhaps' and 'maybe' for Robins in October — 172

NOVEMBER — 177

- What Robins do in November — 179
- Helping Robins through November — 179
- Robin's plant of the month – Common Ivy — 183
- Jobs not to be doing in the Garden during November — 185
- The Night Sky in November — 187
- 'Perhaps' and 'maybe' for Robins in November — 190

DECEMBER	195
What Robins do in December	196
Helping Robins through December	197
Robin's plant of the month – Holly	202
Jobs not to be doing in the Garden during December	205
The Night Sky in December	206
'Perhaps' and 'maybe' for Robins in December	207
The Year's Renewing	210
GLOSSARY	213
Significant Dates on the Calendar	219
INDEX	221
And finally	227

Major Illustrations

'Oi! Where's the sultanas?	16
The last resort. Robins in combat	32
Nuptials amid the myrtle leaves.	47
Gathering nesting material	64
An approximate nesting timeline day by day	72
Full house! Busy robin parents coming and going	82
They're everywhere! Searching for fledglings.	98
The Big Scratch cometh	115
Robin encounters a hedgehog at dawn.	136
Windy days bring surprises.	146
The first Endymion. Robin pondering the Moon.	167
Log feeding station for robins (and other creatures)	182
Eat and be Merry for Christmas has come.	204

INTRODUCTION

Hello again.

Many of my devoted fans, that is those who've read my previous book 'The Magnificent British Garden Robin,' have mentioned how much they would appreciate something like an almanac with lots of information about the nation's favourite bird month by month – all assembled in one, easily referenced volume.

Well, I felt quite inspired when I heard that. So I got pecking away on the laptop once again, just a few lines every day whenever I had time, and I reckon the whole thing has turned out rather well, if I say so myself. You'll find it handy if you want to encourage wildlife to your garden, and especially helpful if you like robins – and, after all, *who doesn't like robins?*

Even better, it has lots of illustrations of me, a really big plus in my opinion. They've all been done by the same chap who did the other book ... you know – w*hat's his name*.

The passing of the months and the cycle of the seasons are important considerations for robins, just as they are for most birds. They motivate our lives and dictate when we build our nests; when we breed; when we moult and even if we choose to migrate (not all robins do). In other words, whether we live in the thickest of wild woods, or whether we live in the most sophisticated and well-tended of urban gardens, we need to be aware of the natural passage of time as a matter of survival.

I expect many of you reading this are gardeners. You love your gardens, and you love your robins, which is perfectly understandable. After all, we are amazing, and very good-looking. But, of course, robins are wild creatures. And if by some curious quirk of fate or negligence your garden were to suddenly return to a wild wooded wilderness, the truth is most of us birds probably wouldn't mind at all.

However – and this might surprise you – we robins do actually like gardens. In fact, in a recent survey, a whopping 87% of robins, when asked, agreed that although they could survive quite adequately in a wild, wooded wilderness, it was much more stimulating and much more *fun* living close to human habitation.

You see, robins are fiercely territorial beings. And when considering a suitable spot in which to live and raise a family, we will always compete with rivals to secure the best. An adequate supply of food; somewhere safe to nest, and a reliable source of fresh water are high on the list of priorities – while a few fruit-bearing shrubs are always welcome during the winter months by way of emergency rations. But there's something more: we also really value a good resident gardener, someone who will be out here with us in all weathers. That's why we follow you

Introduction

about so much when you're working outside. There's always something amusing to see, or some tasty morsel churned up while you're digging and weeding and pulling things about. We will take your presence very seriously when competing with other robins for the best territory. And yes, we will even fight for you as well (I bet you never realised you were such a trophy).

Of course, not all gardeners are suitable. Those who regard gardening as a chore, a bit like housework outdoors, and who are always spraying chemicals and thrashing about everywhere making a terrible din with strimmers, mowers and saws of every description are certainly no friends to robins, or any birds for that matter. That's why there's lots of information in this book about what not to be doing in the garden as well as what you *can* do – because from the perspective of wildlife, leaving things alone is often far better than constantly fussing. This is especially the case if you're aiming to establish a proper wildlife garden – just the kind that robins like best. And if you carry on reading this book, I'll tell you all about that, too: about how you can sometimes just take things easy, do nothing much at all and still reap the rewards.

That's not a bad proposition, is it?

Just a few things to mention before we begin. In these pages, we are looking exclusively at the environment and welfare of the UK robin *(that is, Erithacus Rubecula in Latin)*. And it is also what you might term a Perpetual Almanac. It holds good for each and every year because robins and our ways don't alter all that much from one annual cycle to the next. So it's something you can refer to not just this time around but always.

The sunrise and sunset times given for the first day of each month do vary a little from year to year. Give or take a couple of minutes each way, please.

Finally, you will find plenty of references to berries and fruits in these pages because we robins love many of them. But they might not suit humans. Never eat any berries or fruits gathered in the wild unless you are absolutely certain they are suitable and safe.

January

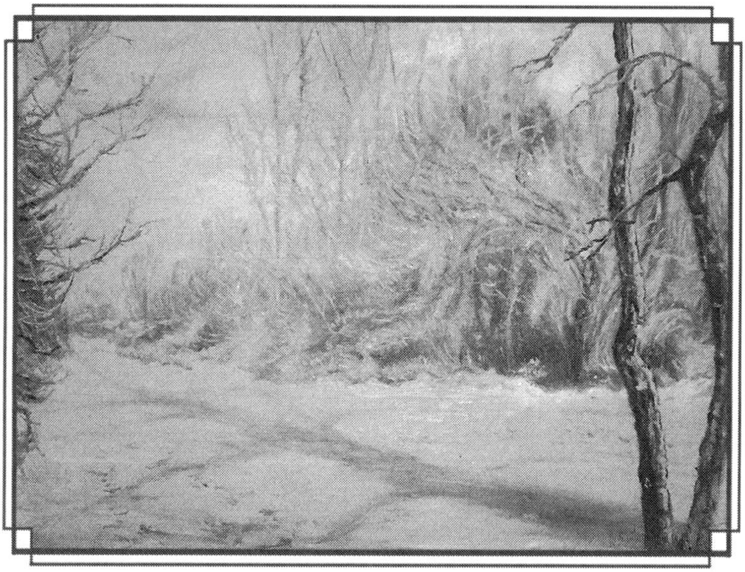

JANUARY

The north wind doth blow,
And we shall have snow,
And what will the robin do then, poor thing?

16th-century nursery rhyme

Most people consider January in Britain as one of the bleakest months. Even though the winter solstice, the shortest day, has been and gone (just before Christmas), the month of January really doesn't feel a whole lot different to the previous one – and that goes for robins and people alike.

In truth, the Sun is getting a bit higher now, just a *little bit* higher in the sky with each passing day, but you'd have to be an astronomer with lots of fancy equipment to spot it happening. Sunset still comes unreasonably early; the nights are still very long, so you'll barely notice any change happening in the length of daylight hours even by the end of the month.

And yes, like the old nursery rhyme tells us, 'the north wind doth blow'. Cold arctic air descends, with snow always possible at this time of the year, especially in the north of the country. Those of a sentimental disposition will tell you that the snowfall is a delight, that it transforms the landscape into a magical world, all silent and slumbering. Yes, very nice, I'm sure, but not exactly ideal for wild creatures like us trying to locate food in the ground. And if there's not a covering of snow, then there's certainly guaranteed to be bouts of frost and freezing rain for most parts, arguably just as challenging. Hard, crunchy soil is a nightmare for birds. And as for finding a nice juicy worm or beetle on the surface waiting to be gobbled up – well, *in your dreams!*

Sunrise and Sunset Times at the start of January

London	8.07 am	4.01 pm
York	8.23 am	3.52 pm
Edinburgh	8.44 am	3.48 pm

What Robins do in January

For all that winter can be a beautiful time, with bare-branched trees lit by the brightest of sunsets, your typical garden robin doesn't have much leisure to stand around admiring the scenery. Instead, you'll find us rushing about, super-busy having to locate and consume enough food to keep that precious spark of vitality burning inside. With only a few short hours of daylight available in which to do this, it can prove a desperate race against time. Just the very act of searching for food on some days uses nearly as much energy as we can ever get from what we find – if we can find anything at all.

So what about the vegetarian option? I mean, are there any berries left to be had on the bushes? Any fruits left on the trees? Well ... in January there might be a few shrivelled specimens remaining, but birds like us (not to mention the hungry mice and voles) have probably consumed most of them by now. So the simple answer is 'no, not a lot'.

Sometimes, when we instinctively calculate that we have enough nourishment to see us through to the morning, we might retire early – that is go to roost – to conserve energy. But then, when we go to sleep and the wind suddenly blows and we get battered by sharp sleet and rain, our survival is hardly guaranteed even then, especially in the case of older birds who are far more vulnerable to extremes. This is a month in which, sadly, many robins will perish.

It's not all doom and gloom, however. Surprisingly, apart from being preoccupied with the search for nourishment, we usually try to find enough time to start establishing (or re-establishing, in some cases) a suitable territory for ourselves. Yes, even at this early stage of the year amid such desperation, we endeavour to stake our claim on a little plot of land to call our own, because if we don't make the effort now, you can be sure other robins will do it for us.

The process of securing territory entails a good amount of singing to advertise our presence and, every now and then, defending our patch against rivals through the occasional bout of aggression. In other words, a handsome, virile robin like me must be prepared to fight, making sure his little spot of land is a suitable prospect for attracting a mate – while a female robin will mark out her patch every bit as vigorously with the intention of perhaps moving in or combining her territory with a nearby male once the warmer weather arrives.

And will she fight? Will she stand her ground and see off intruders? She certainly will – as I've discovered to my cost on more than one occasion. A female robin's beaks and talons are every bit as sharp as those of males. *Ouch!*

Helping Robins through January

This being such an anxious month for robins, we have always been thankful at this time of year for a little assistance from people like yourself. There is evidence that in bygone days, when human society was largely rural, robins used to venture into people's homes during the worst of the winter months. It was an arrangement of mutual benefit, because as well as being offered a few crumbs, the robins would also eat any spiders or insects that might have taken up residence indoors.

I'm not suggesting you do that, of course. I'm sure you don't have too many spiders or insects hanging about in your home anyway, and we would probably make a terrible mess on your carpets. But do please leave out a few crumbs and scraps on the windowsill or bird table if your garden has one (more about that later). Alternatively, and best of all from a robin's point of view, would be to place some morsels for us on a discreet and bespoke robin feeding station.

January

If you haven't set up one of these already, do please consider it now. You see, robins are not your typical gregarious sort of bird that relishes all the commotion and cut-and-thrust of an elaborate bird table – those places where all manner of greedy birds squabble and fight. We are proud creatures, meticulous and independent. So a windowsill, an upturned flower pot in a corner; a log or tree stump – anywhere not too obvious to other hungry creatures – would be just fine. It doesn't matter how close it is to your home, either, as long as it's discreet. Leave a little something tasty there for your favourite neighbourhood robin, especially early in the morning or late in the afternoon. We really need it at those crucial times.

Naturally, you could always go just that little bit further. I'm not suggesting that you put yourself out, or anything like that – but a few exotic items such as mealworms or kibbled sunflower seeds would be quite acceptable in this respect, or, if you can run to it, some raisins or sultanas. Moisten the fruit a little for us first, if you can. Thank you very much.

Here's a handy list of our favourite snacks ...

ROBIN WINTER TREATS

Mealworms (preferably live, but moisten if dry)

Rasins & sultanas (moisten if dry)

Grapes (chopped fine)

Sunflower seeds (kibbled)

Grated cheese (low salt please)

Fat balls or fat cakes (see chapter on February)

Caution: don't leave raisins, grapes or saltanas around if you have a dog roaming the garden, because these can be harmful to them.

Meanwhile, if you are feeling really energetic and the ground is sufficiently yielding, do please get digging. This is the time when you might still be harvesting many of those root vegetables or preparing for next year's crops. And you will be clearing out the old flower beds and borders anyway, making room for new arrivals. That's marvellous, because every time you turn the ground with a spade or fork it unearths tiny creatures for us to eat: beetles; worms; centipedes and what not. Lovely! Without your help, we simply can't reach down in the hard ground to locate them ourselves.

Robins are very fond of sheds. It's not unknown for us to nest in them or even to spend the odd night in them when the weather is bad. So please make sure you don't go blocking up any holes or cracks through which you suspect we might be coming and going.

This might be a good time, also, to consider a bit of tidying and sprucing up inside the man cave or she shed. Give all those grubby sacks and carpets a good airing now, and think about that old armchair, too! Most things that have been gathering dust inside will have lots of spiders and assorted wrigglies lurking within – even if you don't notice them yourself. Placing them outside for an hour or two on a crisp January afternoon is just dandy for robins, and you'll see us hopping about after anything that takes our fancy.

And don't forget the sultanas!

'Oi! Where's the sultanas?'

Robin's plant of the month – the Snowdrop

A welcome sight for many because it's one of the very first plants of the year to bloom, is the snowdrop. It's not purely native to Britain but was probably brought here from Europe, perhaps by monks long ago. The delicate little white flowers on their slender, thread-like stems hang like tiny bells, defying every frost and even popping up through the snow itself.

In popular culture, these early, sometimes premature harbingers of spring, have long been associated with hope, purity and a sense of optimism. They can grow in moist ground and do not mind the shade. And because there aren't too many insects about this time of the year to pollinate them, they rely on their bulbs dividing themselves beneath the ground to flourish. During any periods of unseasonably warm weather, they might sometimes be visited by bumble bees that emerge from hibernation. But you don't go messing with those guys if you're a small garden bird like me. So practically speaking, there's not a lot of interest here for robins. But we love them anyway, the snowdrops. Why? Because we know that *you* do; and also because their subtle fragrance reminds so many other creatures that winter will soon be over.

The Victorians, who were preoccupied with the symbolic language of flowers, maintained that to give someone snowdrops in a posy or bouquet, or even to depict them in art, was considered to be an expression of 'consolation.' Perhaps this was to remind those who were sad or grieving that there was a future still ahead and, just like the season's changing, a potential for renewed happiness. As emblems of rebirth, they also had a religious connotation and were brought into churches to celebrate the annual feast of Candlemas on 2nd February when the church candles are blessed for the coming year

Only do beware: snowdrops should not under any circumstances be picked and brought inside for frivolous reasons. Or so those Victorians warned us. To do so would invite all manner of bad luck and doom to descend upon the family. Snowdrops fail to keep well as cut flowers, anyway, so perhaps there is some wisdom in this gloomy precaution of yesteryear.

These days, numerous varieties of this plant are available, by the way, so you can extend the range of flowering in your garden for months – from before Christmas right through to April.

Jobs not to be doing in the Garden during January

As hinted at in the introduction to this book, robins, and other garden birds are pretty relaxed about you not doing too much outdoors. Naturally, we don't object to you working, planting things and having fun. Far from it. It's just that some folks can – how can I put this delicately? – overdo things a bit and get in the way (sorry about that).

On the other hand, if you would like to become a proper wildlife gardener, and if you would just like to do a little less outside, and try to do it at the right times of the year to suit our natural cycle, you will find us really appreciative. This is what this section of the book is all about and you will find it included for every month. For instance, even now, during the exciting early days of the year, please don't be tempted to trim or clear away too many of those old shrubs or bushes – particularly any that might still have a trace of fruit or some berries on them for us to eat. Old berries and seed heads – even if they might look all rotten and untidy to you, could mean the difference between life and death for a famished robin out here in the wild.

So wait just a little longer please, until the weather turns a bit warmer and the days become just a tad longer – say, by next month. Birds will stand a far greater chance of being able to scavenge for some nice lively food in the ground by then.

The Night Sky in January

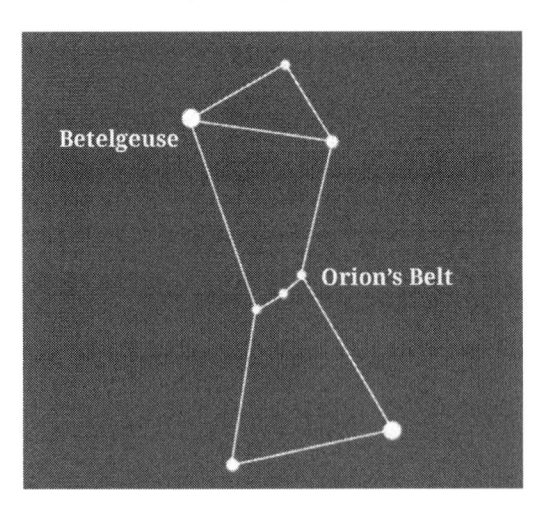

[Diagram of the constellation Orion, with Betelgeuse and Orion's Belt labelled.]

The night sky is important for birds. Robins, for example, if we choose to migrate in the autumn, will fly vast distances, often during the hours of darkness. The night sky is one of those natural phenomena, experts say, that helps us birds to instinctively navigate and to find our way from place to place. Moreover, robins, with our magnificent large eyes, often hunt late into the evening or early in the morning, before the other birds get started. And we are light sleepers, too. We need to be; sensitive always to any vibrations that might signify a nocturnal predator approaching (and there are plenty of those, unfortunately). We even sing sometimes during the night, especially in the presence of artificial light. So yes, we are no strangers to the twinkling of the stars.

All kinds of myths and legends have materialised over the centuries concerning the stars, most of these being splendidly heroic or romantic in nature. And because robins are called upon to be heroic and brave on a daily basis (just as a matter of survival), and because we are also certainly some of nature's greatest romantics, we really do enjoy our stars. Most of these notes assume you have a southerly aspect by which to observe them as they come into view with the seasons.

The evening sky in January, as with most of the winter months, is dominated by the constellation of Orion. A legendary giant hunter of ancient mythology, Orion occupies a large area of the southern sky. Even folks with only a passing acquaintance with the heavens will be familiar with the three bright stars, close together that make up what is called 'Orion's Belt.' In ancient mythology, Orion was said to have been rather on the handsome side, as giants go. And the goddess Artemis, famed as a huntress herself, was rather fond of him as a consequence.

Most of us robins quite like Orion as well, because the constellation contains a very bright star with the appealing name of Betelgeux, which I must say, if pronounced incorrectly (as it invariably is), sounds very tasty. Also, being somewhat on the handsome side myself, and also an accomplished hunter, I have personally always considered myself to have a lot in common with Orion. The trouble is that this chap, as the story goes, was also a bit boastful and full of himself, which is where the similarity ends, of course. He claimed that he could easily hunt down any creature that walked the Earth – an assertion that was always likely to rile the gods. You see, if there was one thing that would really upset the gods of the ancient world, it was boastfulness. The proud Orion's punishment was to be stalked by a giant scorpion and eventually to be stung on the heel, a wound from which he perished.

Robins know all about nasty things sneaking up on them, of course – cats and foxes and so on – another persuasive reason to feel a certain amount of empathy for poor old Orion. The story does have a happy ending, though. To honour the peerless hunter, the gods arranged to have him safely placed on the opposite side of the sky to the summer constellation of Scorpio so the two adversaries should never have to meet again for all eternity.

'Perhaps' and 'maybe' for Robins in January

In nature, there are always annual variations, and the occasional surprise can always occur in timing. Trees coming into leaf particularly early for instance, or certain species of birds nesting at unseasonable times. This section, therefore, towards the end of every month, is all about the 'perhaps' and 'maybe' of the robin world. Not everything always takes place according to the rules. So whenever something is just possible for a robin, even if not entirely *probable*, you'll find it mentioned here. Just in case.

For example, although fiercely independent by nature, robins are also amorous little beasts, and it is always just possible you will find a couple of us pairing up even as early as December or the start of the new year. We might not commence upon the process of mating or breeding just yet (that normally takes place in the spring), but you might just occasionally spot two of us hopping about together, especially if the weather is mild – kind of *rehearsing.* You might also just catch sight of one robin popping a little morsel of food into the beak of another. This is called 'courtship feeding' and we will have more to say about that later on, in subsequent months, when the robin mating season properly gets under way.

Robin Wisdom for January

When the weather is our enemy,
When the clouds tower high above,
Happy is the robin who bides his time,
Recalling days of nests and love.

February

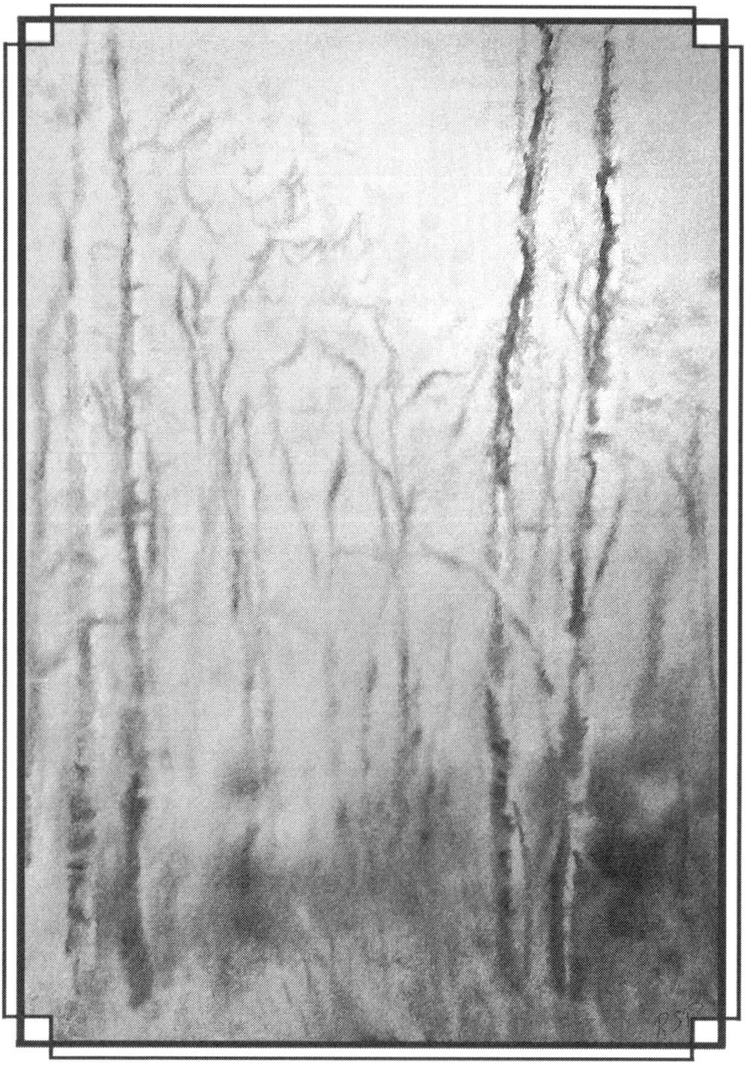

FEBRUARY

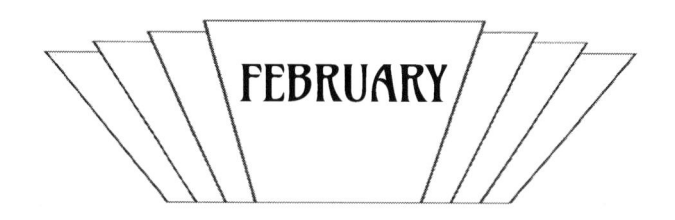

Legend

Robin redbreast is my name,
Of noble legend and of fame.
For courage I'm renowned, and bold.
Yet when the weather turns to cold,
I come to sing beneath your gable,
For a tiny crumb from your kitchen table.

By human reckoning, the month of February is given to be the shortest of the twelve – just 28 days or, in a leap year, 29 days long. This is probably just as well. A bleak month for wildlife and humans alike, no one rejoices in its arrival; no one regrets its passing – and really, the best thing that can ever be said about the coming of February is that it isn't January any longer.

Sometimes, it seems that winter will carry on forever. But, of course, it doesn't. And by the end of the month, the dreary plodding steps of the new year will already have changed into a brisk walk, and the garden is shimmering with the subtle colours of hellebores, winter flowering heathers, daffodils and all the first signs of spring arriving at a pace. There's the opening buds on hazel and alder trees, the dancing catkins on willow and the first signs of violets and fresh wild garlic peeping out from the ground.

Those daffodils, by the way, will still be in flower at least until the end of the month, still full of vigour – and no matter how much it rains or blows you just can't stop them. 'Look at us!' they say, bursting with anticipation. And if you care to listen, you can hear the approach of spring, as well, because by the end of the month our own magnificent robin song is joined by that of other birds like the thrush and the blackbird. And very melodious they are too (even though no match for robins, of course).

Late February into March is, I reckon, a magical time, a few weeks of spectacular and rapid transformation. And we robins find ourselves becoming really very excited by it all.

	Sunrise and Sunset Times at the start of February	
London	7.39 am	4.48 pm
York	7.51 am	4.44 pm
Edinburgh	8.07 am	4.45 pm

What Robins do in February

Although February remains a period when we must continue our desperate search for food, it is becoming a little easier now. And when the milder spells occur, more and more worms and other assorted wrigglies start to appear on the lawns and on the surface of the soil. We know where to look for them, and there is just a little more daylight now to give us time to take our fill before the long night ensues.

Most songbirds, including robins, will have established the boundaries of our individual territories by this time: little patches of land perhaps no bigger than an acre or two and from which, in our case, we try hard to discourage rivals – that is, other robins. Staking our claim to a decent spot that will support our family in a few weeks' time is an arduous process. As stated in the previous chapter, we achieve this to a large extent through the power of song. Robins are messengers of spring. We sing with gusto from a favoured branch or perch and you'll definitely be aware of it – so loudly sometimes, especially if we choose to pipe up suddenly while you go strolling beneath. Ear-splitting. And that, of course, is exactly our intention. We want to be heard, and to be acknowledged far and wide – though, naturally, it is mostly other robins we aim to impress.

Song serves a twofold purpose, moreover, because we not only use it to warn off rivals, but also to attract mates.

Valentine's Day occurs on the 14th of this month, and I know that folks can become rather excited about it: sending cards, buying chocolates and flowers for a special loved one. For robins, however, every day right now is actually a Valentine's Day, and we fetch little gifts and surprise presents to our partners all the time.

During our courtship period, which generally begins around now, if it hasn't already, you might often catch sight of a robin bringing food to another robin. But don't be mistaken. What you are witnessing is not a parent feeding a youngster – that normally won't happen for a good while yet – but rather an adult male bringing a treat, a dainty morsel for a favoured female.

She is, of course, perfectly capable of hunting for food and feeding herself, but this procedure helps to bond us as a pair. Robins, by their very nature, are generous and loving, and what better way to show your affection, I say, than to bring a nice wriggly centipede to the lady in your life! And when you fly up and pop something rare and tasty like that into her beak she will flutter her wings and let forth appreciative tweeting and cheeping noises to demonstrate her approval.

We both strive together now to mark out that little area of home for ourselves, and a breeding pair will take the process of defending their patch from rival robins very seriously. To be fair, actual fighting resulting in injury between robins is rare, and always a last resort. Most disputes are, I'm glad to say, settled amicably through the odd bout of carefully choreographed belligerence – such as loud singing; thrusting our head forward; bobbing up and down; puffing out our chests or flying towards the intruder and swaying from side to side to show off our magnificent physique.

It's actually enormous fun, as long as we don't reach stage 7 in the following list. Until then, we are happy. And that's why, when you hear us robins singing, you may allow yourself a moment of happiness, too.

THE SEVEN STAGES OF ROBIN ASSERTIVENESS

1) Singing

2) Displaying red chest to rival and singing even louder.

3) Swaying from side to side and bobbing up and down where rival can see.

4) Flying up directly in front of rival and repeating steps 1 to 3.

5) Launching oneself almost vertically up into the air in front of rival.

6) Raising talons and sparring

7) Mortal Combat

The last resort. Robins in combat

Helping Robins through February

In anticipation of the upcoming robin nesting season, do please check, if you haven't already, on the integrity of any nest boxes about the garden. Make sure they are securely mounted, clean inside and, preferably, have a reasonable cover of foliage around them to shield us from prying eyes. The female robin will be sitting inside on her eggs for hours every day soon, unprotected and alone, and we certainly don't relish the attention of egg hunters such as magpies, jackdaws or squirrels. So the box should be camouflaged as much as possible.

Meanwhile, if you have a birdbath in your garden, please make sure it remains free of ice because although dehydration is not generally a problem at the moment we still need to preen our feathers, even in winter. Well-maintained plumage helps us stay warm and dry, and we really feel we need to be looking our best right now (see the later chapter on the month of June for details about suitable dimensions and placement for a birdbath).

The end of the month is a good time to finally prune those berry-rich plants, such as elder or berberis. There shouldn't be much remaining on them by way of fruit, and trimming them back now will provide space for other plants to flourish, and also ensure a good supply of fresh berries in the autumn.

Finally, don't forget to keep putting out those scraps for us please – mealworms, fat-balls and so on. Birds in winter aren't too concerned in the way humans might be regarding fatty foods. We just need to *eat*. And fat is an ideal source of calorie-rich fuel for the cold nights.

Fat-Ball Recipe (for cold weather only)

Prepare a dry mixture of kitchen scraps, like crumbs, fruit, seeds, grated cheese, oats etc. But avoid any ingredients high in salt.

Put a few spoonfuls into a plastic container like a used yoghurt pot – fill about halfway – and if you intend to hang up the fat cakes later, then thread a piece of string through a small hole in the bottom of the pot first. Make sure the hole is sealed with something like tape or plasticine so that the string won't slip through.

Carefully heat up a little lard in a saucepan until liquefied, and pour this into your pot(s). Wait for everything to solidify or pop your containers in the fridge. The result will be a unique treat that will certainly be appreciated by your local birds.

Caution: *don't use turkey fat or butter. It doesn't set properly and can get all over our feathers. And don't forget that anything with dried fruit is bad for pet doggies.*

By the way, a handy alternative to yoghurt pots would be to slap some of the semi-cooled mixture into the crevices of a pine cone, which can be easily hung up with string once set. Or one half of a used coconut shell. Be creative – have fun!

Robin's plant of the month – the Daffodil

The bright yellow trumpet flowers that blaze out in the gardens and along verges and grassy banks of the UK in February are the poet's favourites: the daffodils or, as they are more properly called, narcissi. They are so named after the ancient myth of Narcissus, a handsome youth who was tricked into falling in love with his own reflection.

Although the Victorians considered daffodils to be suggestive of kindness and regard for others, a sentiment that lingers on today, of course, it was not recommended that you present a single daffodil to anyone. To do so was considered to bring misfortune. Nice big bunches, though, are always welcome, no matter what century you're living in, and with the miniature varieties available these days they can be included in decorative pots, displayed on window ledges or in conservatories to bring good cheer.

Jobs not to be doing in the Garden during February

I know, with the worst of the winter weather behind, it's a real temptation for gardeners to venture outside and really get cracking, sowing and putting in all those plants and spring vegetables and things. But try to avoid too much drastic clearing and cutting back in those places where you think birds might be wanting to nest. For instance, a semi-wild area in a neglected corner where maybe you found a used nest last year; or a wall or fence covered in ivy that you suspect conceals a popular nesting site. If you cut back now, there simply won't be enough time for a suitable covering of foliage to re-grow around it. In other words, just leave a few wild spots for us in the garden, please – places that will be reasonably safe during the forthcoming nesting period.

And do please refrain from scattering slug or snail pellets everywhere! These can be harmful to wildlife, not just the slugs and snails. Even though the little rascals will be popping up now all over the place to nibble at your tender perennials, it's far better in the long run to let nature do the work for you. Encourage amphibians and reptiles instead, like frogs, toads, lizards newts and slow worms. Establishing a wildlife pond or, at the very least, a boggy area of the garden will attract these valuable creatures (see December). They will consume many of your garden pests brilliantly if you give them time.

The Night Sky in February

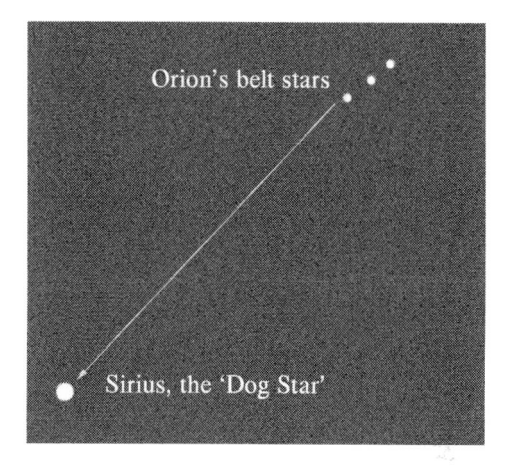

[Diagram showing Orion's belt stars with a line leading down to Sirius, the 'Dog Star']

Way back in the remote and misty depths of time, when Orion was rendered as a constellation and placed in the night sky, he was accompanied by two of his hunting dogs – mostly insignificant groupings of stars really, but one of which, called Canis Major, contains something remarkable: the very brightest star in the entire sky, named Sirius. If you trace an imaginary line down and eastwards through the three belt stars of Orion it will lead straight to the star itself, so you can't miss it.

The name Sirius comes from a Greek term meaning 'sparkling,' and if you ever spot anything brighter than Sirius it will be one of the wandering planets like Jupiter or Mars. Planets (our nearest neighbours in space) are much closer to us than any distant star can ever be. They appear to track their way very slowly across the sky from night to night, and any good astronomical almanac will inform you of their whereabouts. The planets are beautiful and spectacular. But Sirius is the brightest *star.*

The ancient Egyptians were fascinated by this spectacular body, as well as being keen observers of its annual cycle. In fact you could say they were very serious about Sirius. The re-appearance of the star each year just ahead of the rising sun coincided with the annual flooding of the Nile Delta which, in turn, rendered the farming land thereabouts especially fertile. And, as we robins well know, you can't beat a good bit of fertile land since it's always full of tasty things for us to eat.

Sirius certainly brightens up the winter nights, providing it isn't cloudy, of course. But shining in a clear and frosty sky it is a wonder to behold.

'Perhaps' and 'maybe' for Robins in February

Believe it or not, robins can sometimes begin nesting in February, or even earlier! But I should add that this is unusual. It would need to be a really mild spell of weather, or else a particularly reckless pair of robins to attempt it. The daylight hours in which to gather food is still at a premium, and the added responsibility of feeding a nestful of hungry young chicks when so little food is about, invariably leads to failure. The young will not be able to survive a really cold snap, anyway.

For a detailed look at the process of breeding and nesting, see the next chapters on March and April, when the all-important business of starting a family usually begins in earnest for us robins, and is far more likely to prove viable.

Robin Wisdom for February

Young robin lies a bleeding,
No longer the strutting cock.
Vanquished and defeated,
It came as quite a shock.

Be sparing with your prattle,
Be humble in your might.
So when the chains of old age rattle.
You're sure to feel alright.

March

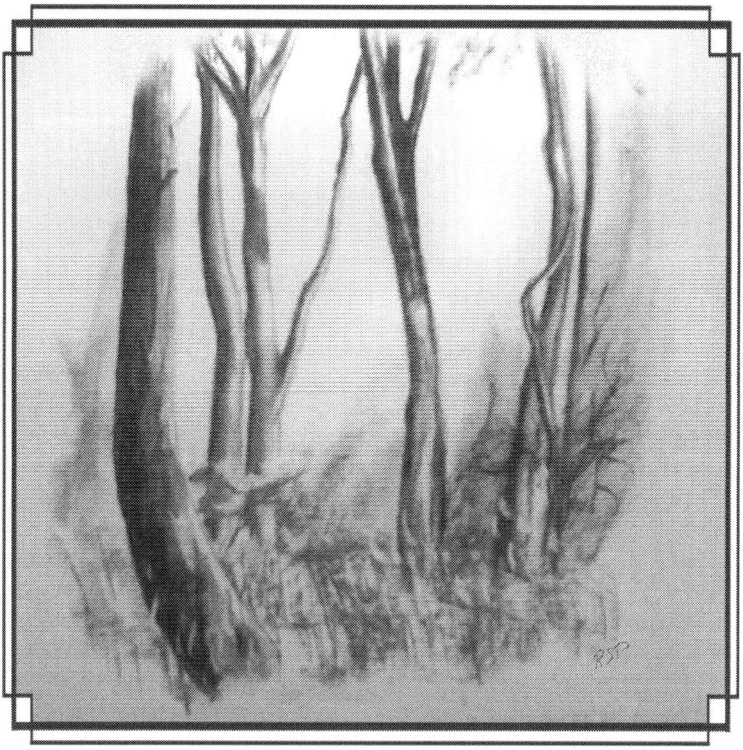
RSP

MARCH

Busy Robins

Beware, other robin.
You shall not come near
Not while I'm busy in March, do you hear?
I shall sing my resistance
If you don't keep your distance.
And never, my friend, shall you see me at rest,
'Til I've pecked you and chased you
From this place I have blessed.

When the daffodils fade, it's tempting to lament that the best is somehow over. We forget how much gorgeous variety of plants are waiting for us in the weeks and months ahead. It will happen. And very soon the yellow daffs will be replaced by so much colour from so many magnificent blooms that you'll wonder what you ever felt sad about. Daffodils are merely a prelude to the great and prolific extravaganza of a typical British garden in summer. Coming soon.

In the meantime, the weather in March can be notoriously unpredictable. And although the blustery winds can be a bother, it's not all bad news, because these will sweep through the garden until all the remaining debris of the old year is finally cleared away. It leaves a special clarity to the air. And the sky, with patches of blue peeping between the racing clouds, has not looked as radiant for months.

I suppose you could think of all this as a kind of 'spring cleaning' on the part of nature: tidying up but on a gigantic scale. And in the place of all that old detritus comes fresh green shoots, vast drifts of youthful foliage across the soil, and a haze of fresh lime-green leaf emanating from trees and hedges everywhere. Primroses pop up with amazing rapidity; blossom begins to show on cherry and magnolia, and the hydrangeas are racing into leaf from their succulent buds as if they simply cannot wait another minute to get started.

Robins feel that way too – we sense how the days are lengthening, and we just can't wait to begin with the all-important mating and reproducing business. It's what we've been keeping ourselves alive and safe for all through the winter. We've arrived at last!

Sunrise and Sunset Times at the start of March		
London	6.44 am	5.41 pm
York	6.53 am	5.40 pm
Edinburgh	7.04 am	5.46 pm

What Robins do in March

Right now, the female robin must prepare for the extra nutritional demands of producing eggs; and males are always hungry anyway. So, in short, what robins do in March is to continue eating. Fortunately after the austerity of winter, there are so many new things for robins to consume that might not have been there formerly – spiders, beetles, worms and wrigglies of all kinds emerging from every burrow and crevice. How very exciting! What a time to be a healthy young robin!

And yes, romance is definitely in the air, or the robin equivalent of romance, which is, I suppose, a little different to that of people like yourself. A robin pair, like most garden birds, will already have noticed each other by this time, and – rather than fighting – will probably have become attracted to each other and bonded as a couple – until now, on the eve of nesting, things will begin to get really serious. A robin relationship is very strong once it gets going. And, with perhaps just the occasional indiscretion – it is one that can last right through to the autumn months and might even be renewed from year to year.

Our foremost aim, however, is to identify a suitable nesting site. It will be the female robin who will choose the spot and who will also build the nest herself. The male robin, meanwhile, and although he might occasionally deliver the odd straw or two to help things along, will otherwise remain occupied with other things, namely guarding the territory and singing. With all that investment of time and energy that goes into nesting (you'll understand what I mean as you read the subsequent chapters) a robin pair will not be wanting to surrender their precious plot of land to rivals. At this stage, they will, if necessary, fight to the death to defend it.

You will continue to witness our special robin courtship feeding at this time, as described in the previous chapter: a gallant little ritual that we really enjoy and which will be repeated again and again throughout the season – the male arriving with a nice juicy item of some kind, and which the female will consume with sounds of delight similar to that made by young robin chicks when being fed in the nest.

Robins are soppy really, and we love all that kind of thing.

Nuptials amid the myrtle leaves.

Helping Robins through March

As the female robin will most likely have been scouting around for a handy nesting site by now, it is vital that you will have concluded any pruning or clearing, especially of climbing plants or ivy. Likewise with the maintenance of any supporting fences or trellis where climbers might be adhering – just those sorts of tempting places where, with ample cover, we might venture to make a nest for our upcoming family.

Not surprisingly, this is also the time when robins are more likely than ever to form a friendship with gardeners. We are so bold and fearless now that you can have us literally eating out of your hand. And if you would like to tame your robin in this way – we really have no objections – start by leaving food close to where you are seated or standing, then gradually indicate that you have the food in your hand prior to placing it down. Over a period of days, you will eventually gain your robin's trust, until he or she will come up and land beside you and eventually onto your hand.

Tip: as mentioned in previous chapters, a few moistened, finely chopped sultanas will usually prove irresistible.

A suitable project for the late winter period and for March, also, is to construct a compost bin. The importance of composting for a wildlife garden really cannot be overstated. Not only will it provide an ideal habitat for a variety of invertebrates, many of which provide food for birds, but it will also be a source of that one magical substance that all gardeners and other creatures benefit from: mulch.

Mulch is simply the end product of organic matter that has rotted, including items such as leaves, weeds, grass cuttings, straw, vegetable scraps and more. In other words, don't waste your garden waste! Your choice of what container or bin you use for heaping it up is not crucial, but ideally it should have wooden walls – planks, for example, secured with posts, and with something laid on top like an old piece of carpet, to keep the heaviest of the rain off. The bottom should be open or in proximity to the soil beneath. Size: a minimum of three-foot square, and about as high.

Best of all is to have two bins side by side. That way, you can move material from one to the other, refilling the first bin once you have transferred its contents to the second where it will continue to break down into compost or mulch within six months or so. This can then be spread around your plants and shrubs to prevent weeds. The more the merrier – especially for us birds since it provides us with endless opportunities to grub around and find beetles, worms and assorted wrigglies beneath.

The mulch, as it decomposes further will also feed your plants naturally. This means far fewer chemicals need to be deployed in your garden.

One word of caution, no matter what design you settle on, don't include unwanted food in your compost bin, as this will attract rodents.

Robin's plant of the month – the Primrose

Primroses can brighten the garden just about any time during the spring, and they can pop up just about anywhere, too. Meanwhile, the range of gaudy, cultivated varieties (polyanthus), which have always been favoured for a quick burst of colour in pots and hanging baskets, remains vast, as any visit to the garden centre will confirm. But you can't beat the sheer delight of those simple pale yellow ones that occur naturally, adhering to walls and banks and spreading in woodland drifts everywhere.

In times past, primroses were highly regarded by country folk because they bloomed at the spring equinox – the day on which we experience an equal amount of daylight and darkness and which usually occurs around the 21st of the month. This pivotal date on the astronomical calendar was known as Ostara in pagan times. A pot of primrose on the doorstep then would exhort the fairies or *little folk* to bless the house, rather than to enter and cause mischief (as fairies were wont to do in those days, apparently).

A little later, the Victorians considered primroses to be symbolic not of fairies but of early youth or the vitality of adolescence. In a peculiar quirk of history, they also became associated with Queen Victoria's beloved and flamboyant prime minister, Benjamin Disraeli, who referred to Victoria herself as his *Faerie Queene*. Upon his death in 1881, she dispatched a wreath of primroses to lay upon his coffin, accompanied by the simple and prominent message 'his favourite flowers.' Ah – isn't that lovely! Just the kind of true story that we romantic robins really enjoy hearing about.

Meanwhile, the date of the Christian festival of Easter, which varies from year to year, is based on the arrival of the first full moon after the spring equinox, a time when the interiors of churches are decorated with flowers, including, among others, the cheerful, yellow flowers of the primrose.

Jobs not to be doing in the Garden during March

If you have a wildlife garden pond, and I hope you will consider having one if you haven't already (see December's chapter), then the time for making structural changes or alterations is over. There might be frog spawn hatching, and the newts, if you are lucky enough to have them, will be coming out from their winter hiding places and taking to the water to breed. The only thing you can safely do with your pond now is drag off any excess weed that might be forming on the surface. Otherwise, leave well alone, please.

Also, try not to let curiosity get the better of you regarding what your robins might be getting up to at such a delicate time. Don't go lurking about, especially near established nesting boxes, peeping in. Also, as mentioned above under the entry for February, leave those shears or hedge cutters alone for now. The opportunity for cleaning or trimming away foliage in sensitive places like this is long past.

By the same token, try not to be tempted into putting up any brand-new robin nesting boxes at the moment in the expectation that they will be used this year. It's too late, and you'll just be wasting your time. We might well be watching you, anyway, and a spanking new nestbox will almost certainly be regarded with suspicion. Next year perhaps, but not this time around.

And please don't go applying any fresh coats of paint or (heaven forbid!) varnish to nest boxes. Even though you might have the very best intentions, any fumes from paint, oil or varnish could well prove toxic to our little chicks when they come along.

Stop fussing! Just enjoy the miracle of spring. Channel your energies into the vegetable patch, or take a nice walk instead.

The Night Sky in March

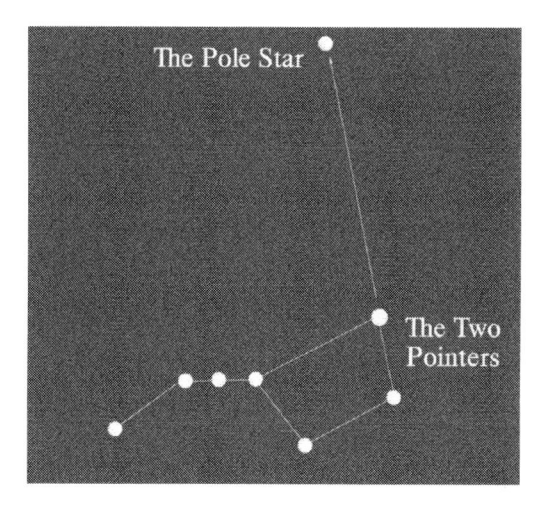

Unlike many of the star groupings mentioned in these pages, the constellation of Ursa Major, the Great Bear – also known as the Plough or Big Dipper – is one that is visible all year round in the UK. Over the course of twelve months, it appears to rotate gradually around what is called the celestial pole, which for us in the UK is situated anywhere between 50 to 60 degrees above the northern horizon.

One of the most convenient of coincidences in life, especially for us birds who navigate over long distances, is that the north celestial pole is occupied by a handy star. Not surprisingly this is called the Pole Star, or *Polaris*, and no matter what night of the year you look for it, it's always in the same spot: about two-thirds of the way up from the horizon and due north. You can locate it easily by using two of the stars of the Great Bear as shown in the illustration. Just follow a line through what are termed the 'pointers' – two stars on the end of the constellation itself and it goes straight to the pole star. So at night, if the sky is reasonably clear, you'll always know which way is north.

'Perhaps' and 'maybe' for Robins in March

British weather is notoriously unpredictable, and especially in northern latitudes of Britain. Spring might be here according to the calendar, but that's not always what counts. In other words, don't be anxious if your robins aren't too enthusiastic even now to be starting on their nests. They *will*, and very shortly – promise. Conversely, as mentioned above, it is also just possible that a pair, with enthusiasm getting the better of them, will have already attempted an early nest in a place you have not been able to observe, a bold but foolhardy venture that has come to grief in the cold.

Nests constructed entirely in the wild and therefore more exposed to the elements than, say, a cosy nesting box against a wall, will be especially susceptible to a period of poor weather. And a prolonged spell of heavy rain can also ruin a nest, despite the heroic efforts of the parents to keep the tiny chicks inside dry.

Don't despair! Robin enthusiasm is irrepressible, and we will try again – *and again* – until we succeed.

Robin Wisdom for March

The plodding old cat on the prowl.
So is robin reckless,
When he seems not to care?

No, not at all,
Neither foolish nor feckless.
For it often does you good,
To indulge in a dare.

April

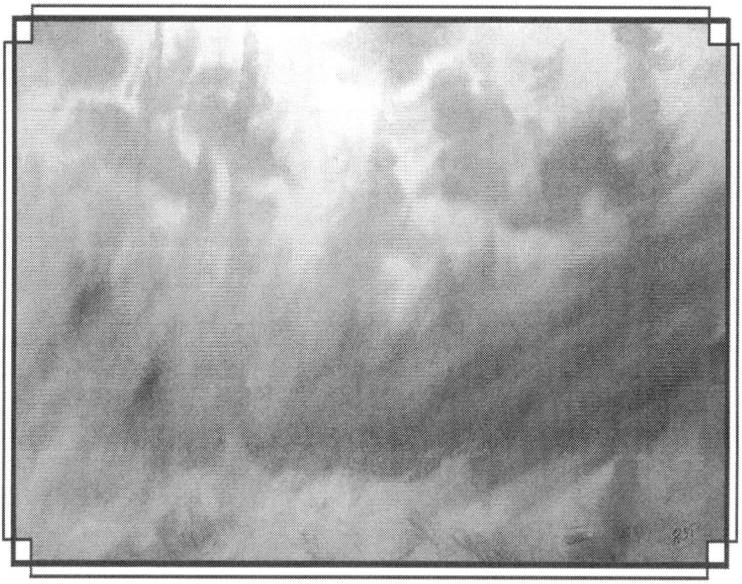

APRIL

Nest

The showers of April pay tribute to the glade,
They make the bright flowers dance and shine.
And a bonny nest with babes shall be made,
If only she will consent to be mine.

Fleeting showers and vigorous tumbling skies are what we expect in April – the month when spring has really got its boots on, striding out. And the natural world is songful, boisterous and full of wonders. No self-respecting tree or shrub will fail to have ventured its first covering of fresh leaves by this stage, silken in texture and often a radiant fresh green. It's all change; and by the end of the month the birds of your locality will have been joined by one or two visitors from overseas: swallows and swifts soaring through the sky. There's an additional company of chattering starlings in the fields and orchards – while in parks and urban gardens everywhere the sound of resident blackbirds and thrushes singing out to one another is louder than ever. It really is amazing, and robins just love it.

Sunrise and Sunset Times at the start of April

London	6.36 am	7.33 pm
York	6.38 am	7.39 pm
Edinburgh	6.44 am	7.50 pm

What Robins do in April

As hinted at earlier, for us robins, the chances of a successful brood of robin chicks coming into the world are so much higher now in April and in May than earlier in the year – the ultimate window of opportunity for raising a family. Put simply, this entails a dedicated routine of mating; building nests, and laying eggs. The male robin is by his nature very willing regarding the first of these three tasks, but it is the female who must now take centre stage for most of the practicalities and all the hard work of making a nest and laying and incubating her eggs.

Indeed, you might already have noticed one of your local garden robins busy gathering nesting material at this time. This will be the female robin at work, and she is searching for a wide variety of materials. Firstly, a supportive base layer of straw, small twigs or dry leaves will be required: the foundation of her nest. Some birds will also pinch a bit of coconut fibre from your hanging baskets if given the chance (sorry about that).

On top of this foundation are woven items of moss, fur, feathers, or even scraps of paper for insulation and comfort. Everything here is moulded into a nice convenient cup shape: soft and springy and wonderfully warm and snug.

Building a nest can take a couple of days, soon after which, the female robin will begin laying her eggs, which she will drop carefully into it – producing usually one per day until she senses that her 'clutch' as it's called of tiny white and brown-speckled eggs is complete. Now she can devote herself to the task of incubation – that is, sitting over them, spreading her wings and allowing her presence to warm and vitalise the embryos within. This must be accomplished without any lengthy interruption. A normal quantity of eggs for a robin clutch is around five or six – though more – in fact, as many as eight – are perfectly possible.

Don't forget, if you see a robin feeding another red-breasted robin at this juncture, it is still an example of the *courtship feeding* described earlier: a male robin feeding a female. This takes place at increasingly frequent intervals now. Moreover, a good, responsible, male robin will also bring food directly into the female's nest during the period of incubation. Courtship feeding is a kind of rehearsal and a pledge of support, therefore, and is often a prelude to actual physical mating, a relatively brief affair in which the cloaca or entrance to the reproductive vessels of the male and female come into contact as the male mounts from behind. During this period, when the female requires male sperm to fertilise her eggs, copulation occurs on a daily basis.

The cloaca, by the way, is a remarkable feature of our anatomy. An opening and internal tube-like formation on the underside of most birds, it serves not only as a reproductive vessel but also a vent for urination and defecation. So it really is a highly versatile organ, and common to both male and female. The male testes, meanwhile, which increase greatly in size and vigour at this time of the year, are housed internally, as well. From here, the sperm will descend towards the cloaca opening, ready for contact with the female cloaca during copulation. In other words, for the gentleman robin, there is nothing external, dangling about and getting in the way of flying. An ideal arrangement, in my view.

By the way, you might be wondering at this stage if it is at all possible to spot the difference between male and female robins by appearance rather than behaviour. The short answer to this question is 'no'. Some folks maintain that one sex is bigger than the other, or has certain markings on their plumage. But the truth is, a lot of these claims will contradict one another. The only distinction at this time of the year is that the female tends to lose some feathers on the underside of her body, the better to conduct her warmth to the surface of her eggs. This is called the brood patch. But it's not visible normally, and once the nesting is over, those feathers grow back anyway.

Helping Robins through April

It may be possible for you to help with providing nesting material at this time, though always bear in mind that robins, like most wild creatures, can prove fickle in this respect. But if you would like to give it a try, do leave some suitable materials in places where you notice the female robin has already been foraging. A little unspun sheep's wool for instance is often very acceptable.

A word of caution, however ... please don't leave out human hair. Although you might well discover traces of hair included among the contents of a used robin's nest, it will usually be animal hair or fur that you see. Human hair, especially if longish, can become tangled in our talons and feet. This is obviously dangerous and can result in infection and pain.

Oh, and by the way, we don't like being followed.

Gathering nesting material

April

So, yes, all contributions gratefully received. Just make sure you don't hang around waiting for thanks. Remember, if you are seen loitering at such a sensitive time, and no matter how noble your intentions, you will look suspicious to us. Robins must be extra cautious now. In other words, if you do leave out material, be discreet – and don't overdo it! We don't need half a sheep's fleece spread out on the lawn. Just a few subtle bits and pieces. We'll find them if we need them.

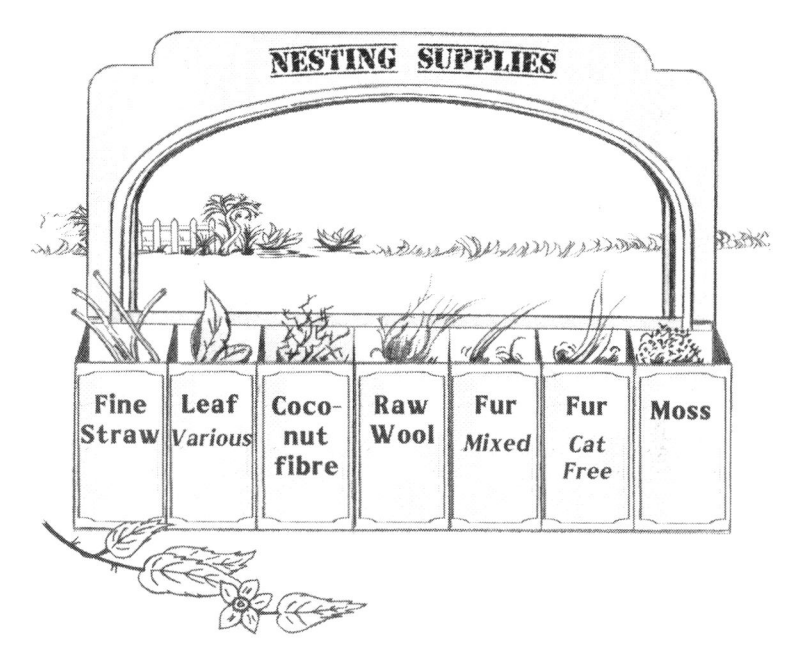

If robins had a store for nest materials ...

Robin's plants of the month – wild Garlic and English Bluebells

Prolific white flowers adorn the woodlands and neglected stretches of the garden in April. These are the wild varieties of garlic. They sometimes occur alongside the flowering of bluebells, making for a spectacular combination. Folks have always used garlic for culinary or medicinal purposes, of course, but it was also considered effective for warding off evil, everything from witches' spells to the unwanted attention of vampires. That must have been a real bonus, I reckon.

Bluebells, meanwhile, were yet another one of the native flowers associated with the fairies. The bells would ring to summon fairies to their gatherings – while the Victorians, with their sophisticated language of flower associations, considered the bluebell to signify the qualities of constancy and kindness.

That is very appropriate, of course, for robins, who are always constant and kind (well ... most of the time, anyway).

We also like wild garlic because it is pollinated by a variety of insects such as hoverflies and even longhorn beetles (a bit on the large size for us). The nectar-rich bluebells, meanwhile – and although served largely by the bumblebee – are also visited by a broad range of other insects. So hungry robins will invariably visit, too.

These wonderful plants enjoy each other's company and can form a rich foundation for the shadier elements of your wildlife garden in spring. So please don't dismiss your wild garlic as weeds. They're not. If you dig them all up, the bluebells will just be lonely, and you'll only have yourself to blame if the vampires come to call.

Jobs not to be doing in the Garden during April

We really would prefer it if you could resist pruning our favourite climbing shrubs such as ivy or honeysuckle at this time, or even cutting into hedges such as privet or lonicera – places that might already have been chosen as our nesting sites. Of course, you will have a good recollection of where those nest boxes from last year are located, (you do remember where you put them, don't you?). But robins, obstinate and choosy beings that we are, might elect not to use any of them, and we could in fact be building our nests somewhere else entirely.

Take a time, therefore, to learn, via a little patient observation, where we have finally chosen to site our nests, and then please leave well alone. It is actually against the law here in the UK to tamper with an occupied robin's nest: a jolly good rule in my opinion.

Due to the horrors of predation, especially among the very young of our species, the average life expectancy for robins is sadly not much more than a couple of years. Even when we reach adulthood, chances are always pretty high that we'll meet a sticky end one way or another. Common causes of death among robins are from cats and wild creatures; from other birds such as hawks; or simply by being careless ourselves, by getting run over by cars, drowning in water butts or flying headlong into windows.

In other words, rearing our little ones at this juncture might actually be a once-in-a-lifetime opportunity for some of us. We can't afford to waste our energy or push our luck on a nest that has already been discovered – one which, from our perspective, is likely to be raided in the near future. Thus, a robin's nest, once exposed or disturbed, will invariably be abandoned. We just cut our losses, move on and start somewhere else (if we have time).

The Night Sky in April

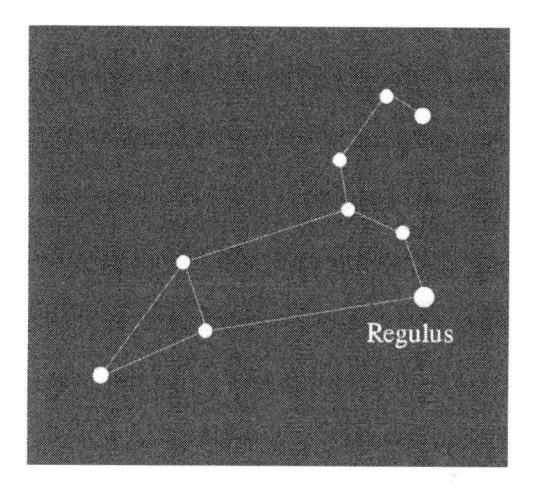

Robins are fascinated by all the old tales from the past, those amazing myths and legends of the ancient world full of romance, heroes and monsters, because our lives are full of all these things anyway. We have to be heroic and brave just to get up in the morning, and we certainly have our fair share of monstrous creatures to contend with, foxes, rodents, hawks and buzzards, on a daily basis. One of my favourite stories is about the origin of Leo, the lion.

Becoming more and more prominent as the month progresses, the constellation of Leo can be detected clearly now in the East, becoming more southerly as the night goes on. Look for its head first of all, like a back-to-front question mark of stars. Once you do spot it, you can never miss it again. At the base of this 'sickle' arrangement is a beautiful bright star called Regulus, while the seated lion's haunches can be detected in a triangle of stars behind, to the east of the sickle.

The lion is no ordinary lion, of course, but depicts the giant mythological Nemean Lion that, long ago, was wont to terrorise the local populace of that region. The mighty hero Hercules was sent to hunt it down – this task becoming one of the legendary Twelve Labours of Hercules. It was never going to be an easy job, though, since the lion was invulnerable, or so it was thought, because weapons could not penetrate its extra-tough hide. Hercules, however, dispatched the monster by wrestling with it, then clubbing and choking it to death. He certainly was a courageous fellow, Hercules.

Although robins are courageous too, I don't think I would have enjoyed an encounter with the Nemean Lion. Keeping out of the way of the neighbourhood cats around here is bad enough, let alone a giant lion.

Anyway – good for you, Hercules! You are rightly honoured, I say, by being depicted in the admittedly rather faint constellation that bears your name. If you ponder the stars here for a moment, you might fancy that he still appears to be brandishing his mighty club, forever in pursuit of the dreadful feline across the sky. A perpetual source of inspiration to us garden birds.

'Perhaps' and 'maybe' for Robins in April

In a good year – that is, a mild one and therefore one likely to provide plenty of food for robins, there might even be young fledglings leaving the nest already and beginning their first adventure into adulthood. More commonly, though, the process of 'fledging' when the young first attempt to fly from the nest is to be observed (if at all) a little later on. See the next chapter on May. Just be aware, however, that it is certainly not impossible in April, earlier than the norm.

Many birds coordinate their breeding cycle, and in particular their nesting period, to chime with other cycles in nature – and robins, although versatile and eclectic in taste regarding food, are no exception. For example, many of our native deciduous trees and shrubs are home to one of our favourite caterpillars which hatches out in the spring just as the buds break and come into leaf. Hawthorn, dogwood, hazels, oak and most fruit trees are regular hosts in this respect, and the coming into leaf of these, be it early or late, can affect our timing with regards to courtship and nesting. Though, to be sure, it is just one of many factors.

Anyway, no matter when we get started, here follows a handy diagram showing the timeframe of robin nesting, from the moment the first straw is brought to the nesting site 'til the magical moment when the fledglings finally leave the nest and a new generation takes wing.

The Robin Almanac

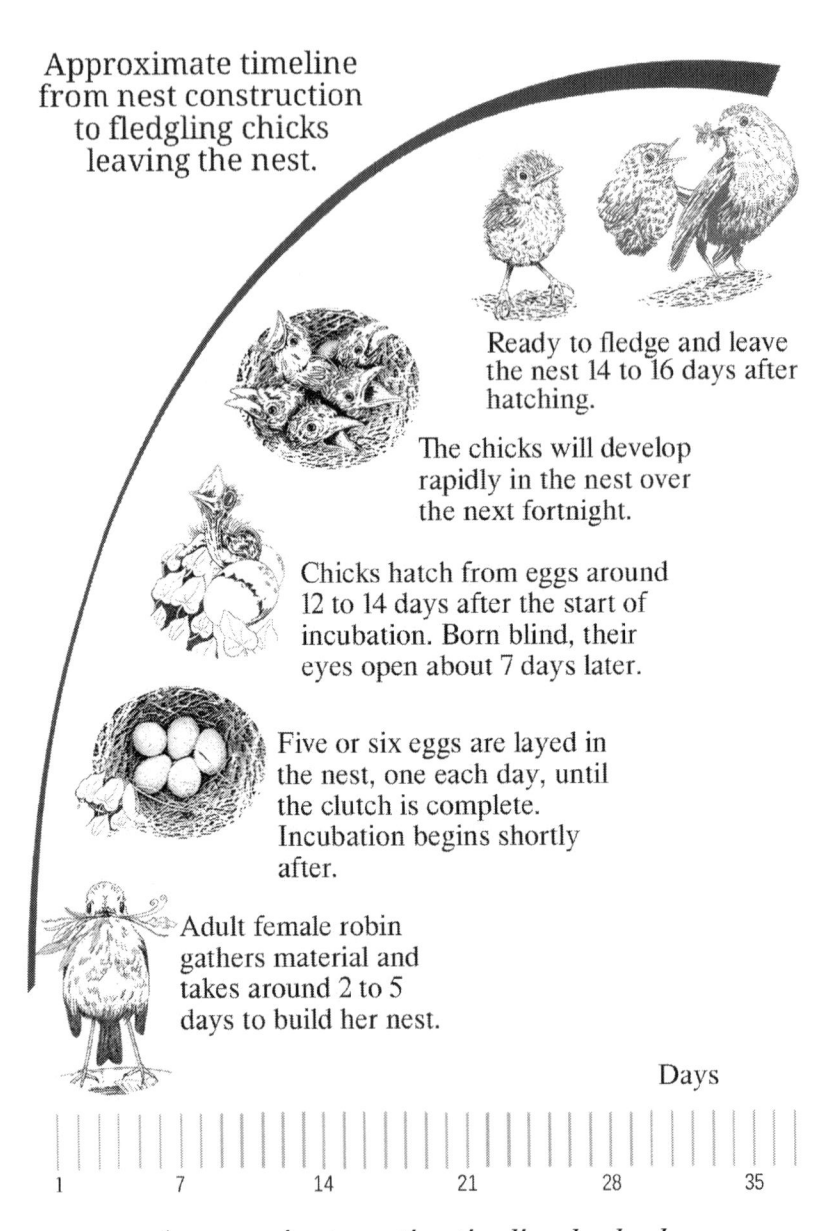

Approximate timeline from nest construction to fledgling chicks leaving the nest.

Ready to fledge and leave the nest 14 to 16 days after hatching.

The chicks will develop rapidly in the nest over the next fortnight.

Chicks hatch from eggs around 12 to 14 days after the start of incubation. Born blind, their eyes open about 7 days later.

Five or six eggs are layed in the nest, one each day, until the clutch is complete. Incubation begins shortly after.

Adult female robin gathers material and takes around 2 to 5 days to build her nest.

Days

1   7   14   21   28   35

An approximate nesting timeline day by day

To sum up, whatever the circumstances or variables in force, you won't see many robins standing still at this juncture. We are on the go constantly and loving every minute of it. And the next month, the merry month of May, is usually even more frantic.

Robin Wisdom for April

You're never lonely in a garden
With a robin,
When he comes up and greets you
A-jumping and a-bobbin'.

And if you share your lunch with him,
You'll have a friend for life.
Through thick and thin he'll be with you,
Through sadness and in strife.

For it's a universal truth
On which you may depend:
That you'll always have chums,
If you've got a few crumbs.

May

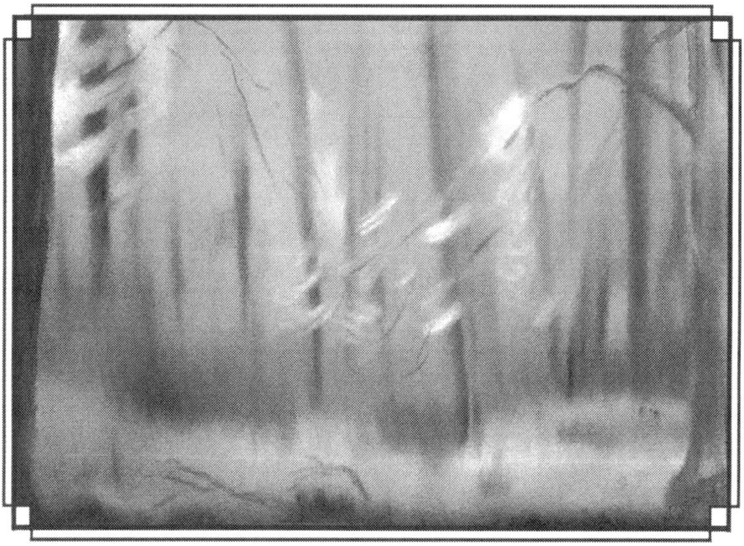

MAY

A Little Something

In May I come a-courting
With a little something in my beak,
To give to my fair robin love,
Who likes to chirp and cheep.
I hope she won't be coy or giggly,
When I show her something nice and wriggly.
In May I come a-courting
With a little something in my beak.

Gardeners and robins alike become really excited at this time of the year as the ground warms and continues to stir with more and more early growth. The beds of tulip and rose are at their most alluring, drawing in regiments of bees, bugs and ladybirds that converge on them from all directions, while the informal stretches display a vast array of colour also: the wildflowers of periwinkle, bluebells, cowslips and forget-me-nots.

Everywhere is greening up. All the trees, each in their own time, will exhibit their full canopies of leaves as the month progresses. Catkins of hazel, alder and willow border the streams and ponds where tiny frogs, toads and newts grow rapidly to adulthood. Frothy white hawthorn flowers border the lanes and pathways. Blossom can be found in every garden, while from the margins of orchards and fields, the cherry, crab apple and chestnut trees, are coating the ground with pastel-tinted carpets of the finest petals.

Everything, it seems, is in a rush, bursting at the seams and competing for space as the very air begins to buzz and hum and to fill with its long-anticipated promise.

Sunrise and Sunset Times at the start of May

London	5.33 am	8.23 pm
York	5.28 am	8.35 pm
Edinburgh	5.29 am	8.51 pm

What Robins do in May

The month of May is one of the busiest times of the year for robins. Chances are we have already located a nest site; built a nest and quite possibly the eggs have already hatched. This means we are working at the double every minute fetching food for all those hungry little beaks waiting back at our temporary home. The illustrated timeline towards the end of the last chapter gives you a notion of just how lengthy the whole process can be. Thirty-six days might not seem like a long time to you, but to a robin it is a minor eternity.

Once incubation starts, and the female robin begins to sit upon her eggs, it takes around 13 or 14 days for the little ones inside to develop and to hatch. Her body warmth and presence is vital here, so she will only leave the nest for a few minutes at a time to forage for food, and often the male robin will bring food to her. As already mentioned, the incubation process is aided by what is called the brood patch, a bare area on the underside of the female robin that enables her body heat to reach the surface of the eggs without the interference of feathers.

As they grow, the embryos inside the eggs take nourishment from the yoke and breathe vital oxygen via thousands of microscopic holes, or pores, in the shell. So they have everything they need to thrive. And they grow very fast. When the time is right, these mighty little chicks-to-be break through the shell from inside, full of energy.

They look a bit odd at first, the hatchlings: little more than a collection of gapping beaks on feet, and totally blind. But we think they are just wonderful, and so we provide them with the nourishment they need to grow – at first a little 'soup' of tiny edible items that we churn up in our gullets and regurgitate for them. But very soon proper items of food can be brought in: tiny bugs; flies; spiders and so on.

About a week after hatching the eyes of the chicks should have opened and they can see us now as well as hear. Consequently, they become very excited and vocal on each occasion when one (or both) of us arrives with a beakful of wriggly goodness. As the days pass, the food we deliver becomes even more substantial, including whole caterpillars and worms until, after about ten days out from hatching, the chicks can take proper adult food. And they have grown so large that they fill the entire nest to the brim.

During this time, you might occasionally notice us hastening away from the nest with a little white package in our beaks. This is the faecal sac – a small item of waste matter enclosed in a membrane that the baby robins produce just after being fed. The sac is integral to nest hygiene, and normally we are present to pick it up and remove it – which we do with care, diligently carrying it to a safe distance so as not to advertise the location of the nest to any would-be predators. Discretion is always an important consideration.

Following a fortnight of rapid growing inside the nest, our young robins might finally begin to venture forth, that is to 'fledge' for the first time and to fly (after a fashion) outside in the big wide world with all its amazing wonders and dangers. We really need to keep a watchful eye on them then, and also to continue to look after ourselves, of course, so that we can fulfil our parental duties. That's one of the reasons why you will notice us constantly cocking our heads and glancing upwards to the sky. Those huge winged predators, the kestrels, hawks, seagulls and buzzards are all hunting for food for their own young now – and robins make a perfectly sized takeaway meal in that respect. Life is dangerous and frantic, and by the end of each long day, protecting and delivering food to the little ones from dawn 'til dusk, we can feel quite exhausted by it all.

Just a final word on robins' nests and the amazing variety of places we make use of. Not for us merely a bush or cleft in a tree or even a box. Robins have been observed nesting inside buildings of all kinds; in post boxes; hats; coat pockets; old boots; abandoned tea pots and saucepans; vehicles of every description, including aeroplanes; and the open pages of a church bible.

The good thing is, almost always folks will suspend any activity that is likely to interfere with the nesting process. This is very much to your credit. And, after all, it is quite an honour, don't you think, to have robins nesting nearby or around your home? We are very special guests. And that is why you feel so proud.

Full house! Busy robin parents coming and going

Helping Robins through May

During such a time of abundance, we aren't all that concerned any longer about food supplies. As mentioned earlier, the juicy caterpillars are hatching out on the trees and shrubs now, and these are ideal for feeding our young. There's a plethora of bugs and beetles, too, and usually the weather is still wet enough for ample supplies of worms popping up from the soil and lawns. Why, we even have some creatures now who advertise their presence – those noisy grasshoppers and crickets that will be out and about by the end of the month and who will be chirping or clicking away for our delight throughout the summer.

This doesn't mean we object if you really do wish to help. The occasional handful of mealworms (our favourite snack, and also perfect for hungry young chicks) still doesn't go amiss. If they are not live mealworms but rather the dried version, please soak them a little first and then place them discreetly, somewhere that won't attract hoards of other much larger birds such as magpies, jackdaws or jays. If we have eggs still unhatched in the nest, these can be targeted by birds like those who will view them as a handy source of nourishment. It has been demonstrated that nests of small birds in proximity to lavish feeding stations set up by well-meaning people in their spring gardens are more likely to be predated by larger birds or even rodents and squirrels. The nearer the feeding station, moreover, the more the nests tend to get raided.

Robin's plant of the month – Hawthorn

Many a hedgerow in our land is constructed in part or in full from the tall flowering shrub we call hawthorn. The popular name of Mayflower is also often applied since its delicate white, five-petal flowers appear now, in this the merry month of May. In ancient, pagan Britain it was bound up with Mayday festivity – or Beltane as it was called, the flowers being a symbol of fertility to be woven into the garlands of maidens during their various frolics and celebrations.

Hawthorn, which can grow to the size of a small tree if left to its own devices, was also believed to possess protective and magical properties and was consequently planted at sites of cultural or spiritual significance. Meanwhile, the old saying ''Ne'er cast a clout till may be out' is urging folk not to throw off any item of warm, protective clothing (clout) until the blossom of the mayflower appears – thus keeping safe from any harsh penetrating winds that can sometimes come as a surprise to robins and people alike as we get carried away with all the joys of spring.

The Victorians considered Hawthorn to be emblematic of hope, even though it was another of those flowers not to be brought indoors. The fragrance attending hawthorn is a bit pungent and unpleasant, so perhaps there was good reason behind this stricture. But outdoors it has long been valued as an excellent hedging plant for fields. As a single specimen, it was also sometimes trained into the shape of a living arbour under which lovers might meet, or even just a handy site to be seated and to converse with chums. Perhaps the arbour was a place where the hawthorn's legendary powers of protection could ward off spies and help folks keep a secret?

> *And every shepherd tells his tale*
> *Under the hawthorn in the dale,*
>
> Milton

Robins, for their part, absolutely adore hawthorn and, perhaps even more so, a very similar shrub in appearance, the blackthorn. They both provide impenetrable cover for nesting birds and for roosting in at night, and the gnarled twigs and branches furnish us with untold varieties of insects, spiders, caterpillars and larvae for us to enjoy. Not only that, but the fruits of the hawthorn – the bright red haws – albeit a bit tough and indigestible for robins – provide autumn and winter sustenance for many birds.

The blackthorn, however, is far more amicable and produces an abundance of soft dark fruits called sloes that can be pecked away at by us birds 'til our heart's content – that is, if folks leave enough behind because the sloes are used to make delicious jams and gin.

A handy tip to distinguish between the two shrubs: the blackthorn flowers come along before the leaves of the tree, while the hawthorn's blossom comes after. So if you come across a nice thorny bush with white blossom but no leaves, that is the blackthorn, whereas the hawthorn flowers are surrounded by fresh young foliage, quite deeply lobed and a little like miniature oak leaves in appearance.

Jobs not to be doing in the Garden during May

Keep those noisy hedge trimmers in the shed, please. The same precautions that applied during April will apply now. Unless you are absolutely sure of where all the various birds' nests are located, don't go cutting and chopping with gay abandon into shrubs and hedges. Even the clamour of mechanical cutters is enough to disturb us nesting birds – let alone having one slicing through the very walls of our home.

Incidentally, no matter how keen you are on your pet cats, please do not encourage them into the garden too often during the daylight hours. I know this seems a bit harsh and unkind, but predation from domestic cats is a major killer of small birds. Millions die every year as a result, and a large proportion of these are robins. Orphan robins whether in the nest or away from it and waiting to be fed are vulnerable little creatures, and even if just one of the parents is killed, the other might not be able to cope with a large family of insistent, hungry mouths. Fledglings are also terribly naïve during the first few weeks after leaving the protection of the nest. They cannot conceive that anything out here would want to harm them. Thus, the advancing spectre of a bewhiskered feline face is regarded merely with mild curiosity, without fear or suspicion – until it's too late.

If we, the parents, are around at the time, we do our best to warn them of any approaching danger, and robin families have a sophisticated set of calls that we exchange with one another for just this very purpose. You might hear some of these yourself if you are in the vicinity – a kind of urgent ticking sound or cheep. This robin 'language' is educational in nature, signifying danger. It can even distinguish between ground and airborne threats. Is it a cat or a hawk?

Eventually, the little ones get the idea and respond appropriately, usually by flying quickly out of harm's way. They will develop their full flight feathers within days of leaving the nest, mercifully, and so have a fair chance of survival thereafter.

The Night Sky in May

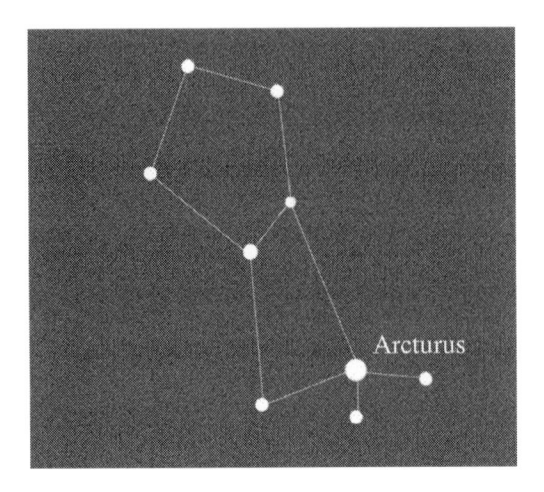

The night sky during the months of spring is dominated by a spectacular orange-coloured star named Arcturus. Unless there happens to be a wandering planet nearby, you really can't mistake it for anything else. Climbing high from the East on evenings in March and April, it becomes more and more southerly and prominent as the night (and the month of May) progresses. Arcturus lies in the constellation of Boötes, and naturally there is a special story associated with this grouping.

In ancient mythology, Boötes – a mortal whose name means something like 'the ox driver' – was a bit of a ne'er-do-well as far as the gods were concerned until, in a moment of inspiration, he became responsible for inventing the plough. His creation was destined to be one of the great early achievements of humankind because, at a stroke, it transformed agriculture and hastened the development of farming and civilised society.

May

Robin would have loved Boötes, practising and perfecting his plough and churning up lots of tasty edibles from the soil along the way: a sort of forerunner of the modern-day gardener. He did well, and the reward for his endeavours was to be honoured by those once-indifferent gods and have himself placed in the sky with his brilliant showpiece, the brilliant star Arcturus, as a beacon for all to admire.

By the way, if you're in any doubt that what you are seeing really is Arcturus and not a planetary interloper, you can check by locating the Plough or Great Bear constellation once again (see notes for the night sky in March). Follow the curve of the handle or tail and trace an arc downwards, some distance across the sky to the star itself. You might then be able to imagine a kind of torso-like shape in the surrounding stars, like the top half of a human body, busy driving his oxen across the sky.

Remember, you can always check with your favourite astronomical almanac for the precise locations and movements of the planets, which are different every year.

'Perhaps' and 'maybe' for Robins in May

In the event that we began nesting early this year (see notes on the previous month), and the chicks are already fledged and away from the nest, then I can assure you we remain every bit as vigilant and busy in the parenting department. We are rushing around fetching food for them still – and in fact will be for several more weeks to come until they can fend for themselves. They might be hiding up just about anywhere now within our territory, waiting in the undergrowth or in bushes for food, so in a way we are compelled to work even harder than ever now, just to find them!

Not only that, but sometimes our enthusiasm gets the better of us, and we might even be considering another brood – admittedly a tall order now because our duties to the earlier youngsters and any new fledglings that come along will overlap. Even worse, robins can sometimes be bigamous, that is an over-amorous male will occasionally venture a partnership with a second female and begin an additional brood elsewhere. Now I couldn't possibly comment on that sort of behaviour, but I understand from robins who've partaken of it that it really does entail a considerable amount of extra work. So not to be recommended.

Mind you, that's nothing compared to some other bird species I know of. My friend the wren says that, in their tradition, it's the *male* who builds the nest rather than the female. And not just one nest. He reckons it's normal to go around building half a dozen 'cock nests' for his lady. These don't have any lining yet but exist merely as a selection of what you might term 'unfurnished' residences. His favoured lady wren then inspects them and chooses which one she likes best, taking charge of the interior décor herself, lining it with feathers, fur and such like, according to taste.

Well, I think that's a bit over the top, don't you? I'm glad I'm a robin and can just concentrate on singing while Mrs Robin builds the nest herself and sits on the eggs for weeks on end. A far better arrangement.

(Isn't nature wonderful!)

Robin Wisdom for May

When the nest is full of babes,
And we work with tireless pleasure.
We know one day they will depart,
And memories be our treasure.

June

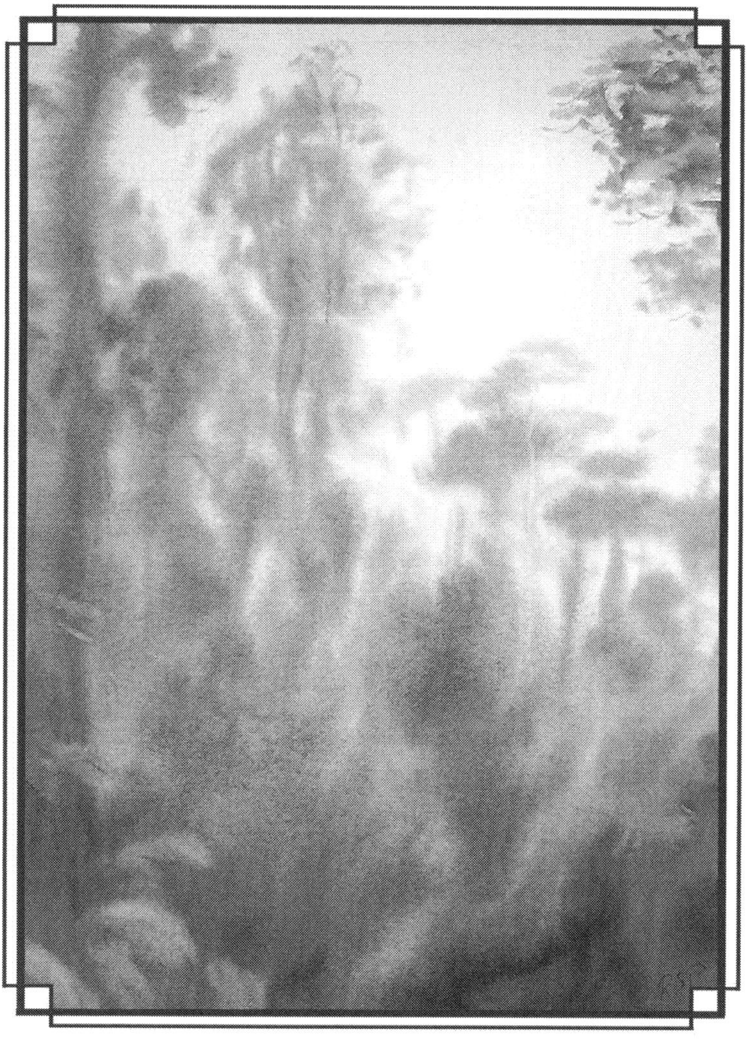

JUNE

Dawn Chorus

At dawn there's such a terrible din,
With all the other birds joining in.
I can hardly make myself heard.
Noisy, noisy, noisy bird!

The longest days of the year occur now at midsummer; the hours of darkness brief. Gardens are lush with bloom. And clematis, fresh ivy and purple-flowering wisteria grace the walls. The melodies from us birds reach a crescendo of excellence, and the exultant dawn chorus is rightly proclaimed as a thing of glory. Even by day, the robin must compete to be heard since other birds are as busy as we are and every bit as vocal. And then, after dusk, in certain favoured places, the robin meets its greatest rival in song, the nightingale, a summer visitor to the UK and who, like us can be heard singing even in the dark – only not just spasmodically as might a restless robin roosting near a street light, but rather by its very nature steadfastly through the darkest of nights.

The variety of wild food in the garden is almost overwhelming – caterpillars; beetles and bugs; thrips and flies, and spiders of every shape and size – while down there in the soil, the countless millions of worms, centipedes, millipedes and the lava of a myriad insects add to the lavish variety on offer for a peckish robin. Trouble is, these also tend to draw the presence of larger creatures who feed on them, too – rodents, frogs, snakes and even in some parts of the country badgers – not to mention some of the more troublesome birds like magpies, jackdaws or crows. And even though there is certainly enough to go round, some of these creatures will still insist on raiding our nests if they can and eating our eggs. Disgraceful.

It's all a mystery, isn't it? Why, for us to live, should something else have to die? 'What *is* it all about?' a robin might wonder for a few moments of profound introspection before hurrying off for lunch. Perhaps it's all to do with the great 'chain of being' that ancient peoples once considered to exist everywhere, linking all things in a structure of mutual need from the tiniest and most humble up to the very greatest. Whatever it is, it's surely evident in June, when the Sun is at its highest elevation in the sky, beaming down upon the ultimate demonstration of nature's abundance and complexity.

Sunrise and Sunset Times at the start of June		
London	4.49 am	9.08 pm
York	4.30 am	9.35 pm
Edinburgh	4.35 am	9.46 pm

What Robins do in June

As mentioned in the previous month's notes, a second or even a third brood could be underway at this time, especially if a robin pair are feeling particularly confident. But often their enthusiasm will be due to previous attempts at rearing a family that have failed or been hit by disaster, and they simply wish to try again.

However, looking on the bright side, as all robins must, if things have gone according to plan, our own little ones are well and truly fledged now – that is, they have developed enough in the nest to spread their wings and enter the big wide world. Unfortunately, they are not able to fly properly for the first few days, so we encourage them to lie low in various parts of the garden, preferably in places where they will not be detected by foes. But they are only young, and inclined to roam. When we arrive with food we find them having strayed into all sorts of peculiar places.

They're everywhere! Searching for fledglings.

Helping Robins through June

Although nature supplies us with plenty of food now, and robins really don't need too much support in the culinary department, what we really do appreciate is a regular and reliable supply of fresh water. During hot and dry weather any standing water that we might use for bathing or drinking can evaporate and disappear pretty quickly. And stagnant waters in ponds and ditches in the wild, without rainfall to replenish them, can harbour mould, bacteria, parasites and lice. All these can prove a terrible inconvenience to robins at the best of times. At the worst, such horrors can prove fatal.

So, if you haven't done so already, please consider placing a birdbath in your garden. We love bathing. Even a humble bowl or upturned dustbin lid will do as long as it's kept topped up with fresh clean water.

So what makes for a really good birdbath? Well, to begin with, it will feature a substantial basin, wide enough for a bird to spread its wings and splash about inside, say around twelve inches wide. And it should not be overly deep. For a robin, that means it should never be able to contain water to more than a depth of about two inches at its centre – more shallow on the circumference, of course, with sloping sides.

The basin itself should rest upon a plinth of about two feet in height so as to be out of range for ground predators while affording the birds who use it a good view of any impending jeopardy. Birds are naturally very cautious and nervous when taking the plunge since being all wet and half-submerged can be a vulnerable few moments for any creature. The plinth itself can come in all shapes and sizes, and with all kinds of fancy designs, too, so you can always find one that suits your style and your garden. So what are you waiting for? Pop down to the garden centre and choose one. It will last for years, and that way, you'll be able to watch your local robins, and other birds splashing around just about any time, including the evening before we fly off to roost.

Meanwhile, planning ahead a little, think about finding a little space in the garden to plant out some berry-rich or fruit-bearing shrubs that will provide food for birds like us in the autumn and winter months ahead. Any of the following are suitable:

> Blackberry   Blackthorn   Blueberry   Elder
> Hawthorn   Holly   Honeysuckle   Ivy   Pyracantha
> Spindle Tree   Sweet Briar   Wild Cherry

During these early days, keep any new bushes or saplings well watered – especially during any dry spells – and in fact it is a good idea to keep an eye on them all through the summer anyway, making sure they are properly bedded in. If you have invested in fairly mature plants, they will bear fruit within months, full of vital sweetness, vitamins and minerals to sustain us during the barren season of winter. Believe me, those days will come soon enough!

Robin's plant of the month – the wild rose

By 'wild' rose, I mean non-cultivated examples such as the Eglantine or the Dog Rose. Both are native to the UK, and they make ideal hedgerow plants. Even a single specimen will provide birds like us with a rich source of insects, caterpillars and bugs at just the time when we need them most to feed our babes throughout the summer.

The flowers of the Eglantine or, as it is more commonly called, the 'sweet briar', are usually a splendid red colour in summer. And the resultant fruits, although a little on the large size for robins, provide a rich source of vitamin C for birds and wildlife during the early winter period. Many of the fine, cultivated roses you find in gardens the world over are descended from the sweet briar or similar. Robins love wild, rambling roses like these because they present another one of those fierce, spiky barriers to predatory animals. The razor-sharp thorns are no hindrance to robins, however, who can weave between the branches of the dense thickets with consummate ease. Consequently, wild roses are ideal for nesting and for roosting. We love them.

Folks have always associated the Eglantine rose with the qualities of purity, romance and devotion, and across the centuries it has consequently been beloved of poets and artists. It was a favourite with Elizabeth I, and has also found itself immersed in Christian iconography. So it really would be challenging to find a plant more appropriate for the likes of passionate red-breasted birds like us. If Eglantines had wings, they would surely be called *robins.*

Jobs not to be doing in the Garden during June

With every plant, and every weed growing so fast right now, it's tempting for gardeners to want to go on the offensive. But do avoid overreaching in the toxic chemical department, please. Many commercial weedkillers or pesticides contain compounds that can be harmful to wildlife, especially if used incorrectly (that is, usually applied too frequently or mixed too strong). Baby robins are fed on worms, caterpillars and other assorted wrigglies that we find in the very lawns you might have chemically treated, or upon the stems and leaves of plants that you think of as weeds worthy of destruction. So at the very least, please read the instructions carefully, and use responsibly and, above all, *sparingly.*

Alternatively, these days, you might want to investigate the range of natural solutions that can be purchased at garden centres. The practice of using nature to control pests will often call upon the services of microscopic creatures called *nematodes*, which possess all sorts of special characteristics. They will destroy pests such as vine weevil in the summer or leatherjackets in spring and autumn and will do so in a completely natural way. They are perfectly safe to put in the path of birds; and also safe for pets, children and wild animals alike.

Regarding robins specifically, meanwhile, in addition to not spraying so many chemicals over our food, please try to desist from thrashing about around places where young robins might be hiding. As mentioned previously, our fledglings cannot fly at all well for the first few days after leaving the nest, which is why we keep them sequestered in bushes or in patches of dense undergrowth.

We still communicate with them regularly via various calls and we know where they are (most of the time). But chances are *you* won't, so please continue to exercise caution when you are busy or in a hurry. Children included. And if you happen to come across a little speckled baby robin (it won't have any red breast yet) standing alone in some secluded place in the garden, please don't touch it. It will almost certainly NOT have been orphaned or abandoned, as you might assume. It is just waiting patiently for its dinner.

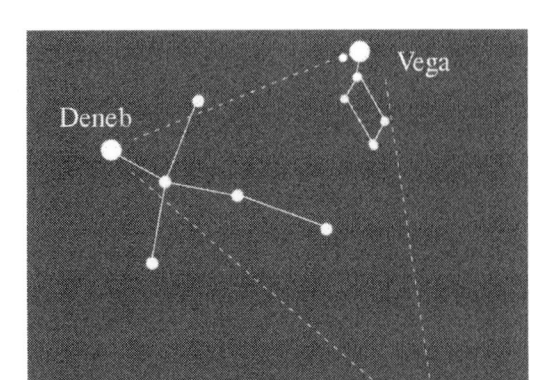

The Night Sky in June

The height of summer – that is the longest day and shortest night – occurs during this month. Our continental robin cousins and their gardeners mark this with the Feast of St John on midsummer's eve, round about the 21st of the month, when bonfires are lit, bottles are opened and a jolly good time is had by all. Here in the UK, meanwhile, folks observe their own unique festivities on warm mid-summer evenings with smoky barbecues and sausages.

With such short nights, the sky is never truly dark for very long before the early dawn arrives just a little ahead of 5 a.m. But you can still see a magnificent triangle of bright stars after sunset if you care to look – what stargazers term the Summer Triangle – and which also contains two star groupings named after us birds, albeit pretty large specimens: the Eagle and the Swan.

Did you know that stars have colours? These are subtle variations, naturally, but you can train your eye to see them. And the Summer Triangle is a good place to start. Almost overhead, for example, you'll find the brilliant star named Vega in the constellation of the Lyre – diamond-like and, as stars go, distinctly blue in colour – while across and down a little towards the East on the opposite point of the triangle is Deneb in the constellation of Cygnus the Swan.

Deneb has a faintly yellowish hue, and it is easily identified from its surrounding stars, which, along with Deneb itself, forms a distinctive cross formation. Indeed, the constellation of Cygnus is sometimes referred to as The Northern Cross.

Meanwhile, the bottom corner of the triangle can be located down a ways towards the southern horizon where you'll find the bright star Altair, almost as bright as Vega but without the blueness. So, you see, the triangle itself covers a large area of the southern sky, wheeling from east to west as the night progresses. Altair, meanwhile can be confirmed easily because it is flanked by two other conspicuous stars – helping, all together, to depict the heart and wings of the constellation Aquila, the Eagle.

How many other stars can you spot that have a distinctive colour to them?

'Perhaps' and 'maybe' for Robins in June

Robins tend not to use the same nest more than once, and by the end of the month there is only a low probability that we will be building new nests and starting a fresh brood. But bear in mind, it could and does happen *sometimes.* Even now, if you chance unexpectedly upon a nestful of small whitish eggs as you go about your business in the garden, please don't necessarily assume it has been forsaken. Treat the area around it with respect for a few more weeks still to come. Robins and their nests are protected by law here in the UK. And that's not a bad thing, in my opinion.

In other words: *Do not disturb!*

Robin Wisdom for June

When summer's plenty sets us free,
In the bounty of leaf and fern,
Wise birds will humble be,
And think on fortune's wheel,
That does not cease to turn.

July

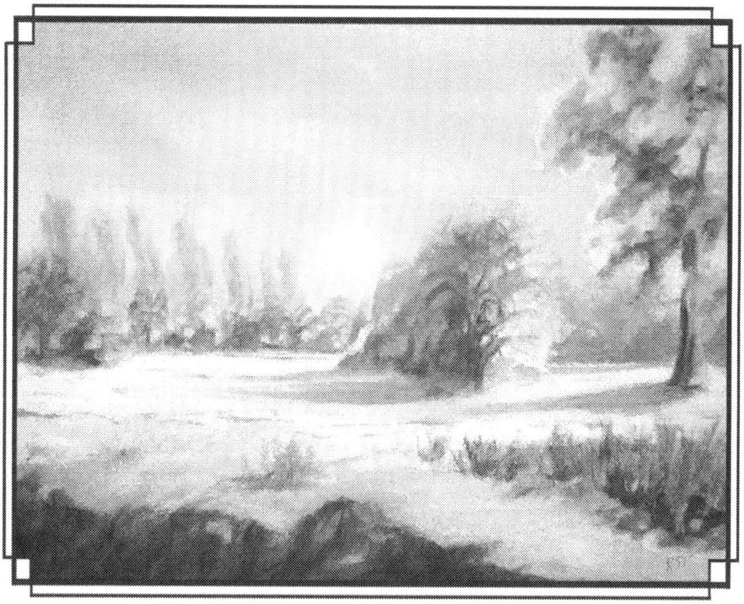

JULY

If I

If I, a robin, could a skylark be,
I would take me high up to the sky.
And all the world below me I would see,
And happy, I would be,
To fly and fly and fly.

The richness and variety of the natural world in July is almost overwhelming, the very air full of vitality. It includes now the beguiling chatter of skylarks from the open heath as they ascend higher and higher into the sky, their ceaseless twittering replacing the no-longer quite-so exultant song of our native songbirds - which apart from that of robins, will have faded entirely by the month's end.

Meanwhile, in that same once empty sky, frantic swallows and swifts continue to dart this way and that, catching flies on the wing, while the ravenous falcons, kestrels or hawks, hover, or perch menacingly, their eyes scanning the garden for any sign of prey – anything from a vole to a song-bird chick that they will seize in their sharp talons and carry away to feed their own hungry brood. Even a frog; even a cricket isn't safe out here!

The walls and verges of the country lanes are crowded with all manner of wildflowers, pink mallow, golden rod and purple loosestrife all striving upwards in endless competition for light and space. In the cottage garden, the long stems of the foxgloves and lavender stoop heavy with bees drunk on nectar; while the formal beds and parterres of stately houses are resplendent with roses and assorted summer glories whose multitudes of names are sometimes too much to remember even for the gardeners who once planted them.

With the days seeming to become ever warmer, there remains ample resources and nourishment for all living things. The crops in gardens and allotments are abundant, and soon the harvests with all their hoped-for plenitude will be underway in the fields and orchards. There is a sense of repletion; of time standing still as robins approach the final phase of our annual breeding cycle.

Sunrise and Sunset Times at the start of July

London	4.47 am	9.20 pm
York	4.36 am	9.39 pm
Edinburgh	4.31 am	10.01 pm

What Robins do in July

Although parental duties still predominate in the life of a typical adult robin, and will do for much of the remaining summer, the heaviest of our responsibilities are gradually winding down now, and by the end of the month we should expect to find ourselves with just a little more leisure.

You might be wondering why robins are not inclined to continue breeding at this time; to just carry on; build another nest and have yet another brood of chicks? After all, we have a good few months more of warm and clement weather ahead, and ample supplies of food available to nourish our offspring. But, in fact, it's rare to indulge in more than three broods during any one season, because even if we do try, there are certain factors that will limit the potential for success.

For a start, our juvenile robins, as the little ones are called during their first few weeks out of the nest, still need looking after during the summer months. They have to learn to fly properly, and even then, with all their new flight feathers fully matured, they will still expect to be fed by their parents for some time to come.

And there is also one other very persuasive reason to curb our enthusiasm. It's approaching that time of the year that heralds the onset of one of the most traumatic and unsettling periods of a robin's yearly cycle: the dreaded moult – that uncomfortable but entirely necessary annual event in which our feathers simply begin to fall out. I really don't look forward to this at all. Our old feathers are replaced by new ones, of course, but it all takes a long time, making for a challenging and sometimes hazardous period for us proud robins (see the upcoming chapters on August and September). At such a time, therefore, we prefer to just keep a low profile and not to be conspicuous.

And if that wasn't enough to contend with, we are also afflicted now by an equally uncomfortable bane of summer: those nasty infestations of lice and fleas that make themselves at home in our plumage and which no amount of scratching, bathing and preening can ever seem to shift. We can also succumb to fungal infections, especially around the eyes – horrible.

All these factors combine to make a mid-summer brood somewhat unlikely, and it's often more than enough for us just to take care of those we already have, guiding them towards becoming proper little adults themselves in time.

July

The Big Scratch cometh

Helping Robins through July

Here in the UK we usually find ourselves facing the driest of seasons now. July and August have scant quantities of rainfall – so low in some parts of the UK that the term 'drought' often features in the weather forecasts. These are conditions that could persist for weeks at a time. The farther south and east you are in the UK, the more likely this is to be a problem, and it can make life for birds very difficult, too.

That's when that birdbath becomes literally a lifesaver. Although we obtain moisture from the food we eat, dehydration can become a peril for just about any creature now. Summer months see a very fast evaporation of water, and you probably realise, I hope, that the birdbath needs to be topped up regularly, more or less every day at this time of the year. But something else also needs to be kept in mind: reliability. It's no good having a nice birdbath full of fresh water if you suddenly go away on holiday and are unable, therefore, to replenish it. Your local birds might well have come to rely on your beneficence, and it can be upsetting when the water is no longer there and we are obliged to search elsewhere, desperately seeking alternative sources.

If you have a kindly neighbour who comes in to water your plants when you're away, perhaps you could ask them if they might top-up the birdbath too?

Robin's plant of the month – Honeysuckle

You might expect a robin to choose the most majestic of all flowers, the lily, as July's flower of the month, but the beautiful lily cannot compare in practical value or longevity of bloom to another of our all-time favourites, the honeysuckle. This delightful climbing plant comes in a good few variants, from the wild, native version with its cream flowers which turn yellowy with a little pink mixed in, to the many different cultivated, garden varieties that have a broader range of colours. Robins, however, love the wild woodland honeysuckle best – ideal for foraging, nesting and for the glossy red berries later in the year. (Don't eat them yourself! They don't suit humans, but we birds can tolerate them well).

In the past, folks used to believe that a good fragrant honeysuckle growing around the front entrance or porch of a home would ensure good fortune for its occupants, while also warding off any baneful influences. Good vibes, in modern parlance. In the works of Shakespeare it was referred to as the woodbine, a plant representing devotion. Later on, the Victorians became equally stimulated by its clinging nature because it reminded them of romantic attraction and fidelity. Its scent, however, they believed, was far too sensuous to be brought safely indoors, especially if there were young ladies in the house. Alternatively, and possibly due to its perceived stimulating nature, it also became associated with inconstancy in love.

Not only will honeysuckle probably still be flowering in September, but it is another one of those plants that's a real draw to insects, spiders, moths and butterflies, so a must-have addition to any respectable wildlife garden.

Jobs not to be doing in the Garden during July

Try not to go pruning those lavender bushes so early. A time-honoured piece of gardening wisdom tells us that if you want nice subtle lavender plants next year, you should prune them soon after flowering. Some folks are so devoted to this idea that they seem to prune them back long before even then! If you really must prune so eagerly, perhaps you could just allow a more mature and lanky lavender bush to flourish somewhere else in a remote corner of the garden. Give it a chance to run its course through all the summer months. The stately English lavender, for instance, can still be an attraction and food source for bees and other valued pollinators as late as September or even beyond. I'll have more to tell you about this wonderful wildlife garden plant in the next chapter, in August.

July

But for now, here next is a subject dear to the heart of garden birds everywhere: Soft fruit.

It's a delicate one, I know. And robins, as well as being partial to a little soft fruit ourselves, are also realistically minded creatures. So I suppose there's not much point in suggesting that you desist from erecting cages and nets and other protective barriers around your succulent vines and strawberry beds to keep us birds out? No. That's a given (unfortunately). But do please keep a watchful eye on your nets in particular. Birds, especially robin-sized birds, can become tangled in them or trapped behind and then they will dehydrate or starve (there's only so much soft fruit you can consume, even if you're a robin).

I suppose the truth is, we really don't approve of nets at all, not in any shape or form. In some parts of the world people once used to catch robins in nets deliberately and then either put them in cages or eat them! How's that for bad behaviour? So you can imagine how easily it is for us to come to grief in any kind of mesh.

By the same token, in your enthusiasm to protect your garden produce, please don't leave any rodent control measures exposed in places where birds might venture. We can perish easily in mousetraps. If you must use them, pop them inside an open-ended tube of some kind.

The Night Sky in July

Have you ever wondered about that faint and narrow band of what looks like high-level cloud or dust stretching across parts of the night sky? That is what's called the Milky Way – and it's made up of millions and millions of distant stars. If you take a look at the night sky on a clear night in summer and give your eyes a few minutes to accustomise to the dark, you will notice it easily. The only hindrance to obtaining a clear view of it (apart from cloud, that is) is the glare from streetlights or the presence of the Moon.

The Milky Way is actually a view of our own vast galaxy of stars edgeways-on from within. And during evenings in July it can be seen to traverse the territory of the 'summer triangle' you met with in the previous chapter. The course it takes passes some distance beneath the bright star Vega and then down through the Swan and the Eagle. If you have a pair of binoculars handy you might be able to distinguish lots of individual points of light along the way. The higher the magnification, the more individual stars will be resolved. You can observe it at any time of the year, but in summer, on a good night, passing overhead from one horizon to the other, it really is spectacular.

'Perhaps' and 'maybe' for Robins in July

Although I have told you earlier about the various restrictions that might discourage us from commencing upon another summer brood, it is not entirely unknown for robins to mate and continue nesting late into July. Examples have even been recorded of robins rearing a successful family as late into the year as August.

Moreover, in the unfortunate instance of an entirely infertile clutch of eggs, it is also not uncommon for a female robin to continue to sit on them and attempt to incubate them long after the eggs have passed any realistic chance of hatching. Examples have been observed of this broody behaviour continuing for as long as four weeks after the normal incubation period until the poor robin finally gives up and calls it a day. These misfortunes tend to be the exception, of course. But you should still be prepared for them and continue to exercise caution in the vicinity of nesting sites until the final window of opportunity closes with the onset of autumn.

Robin Wisdom for July

Now is the season of danger,
From fox and hawk and cat.
Our babes have so many foes,
Threats and hurts from this and that,

A robin's life is short, it's true,
But that is nature's way.
Fear, thus, no more the fox or hawk,
Than the passing of a day.

July

August

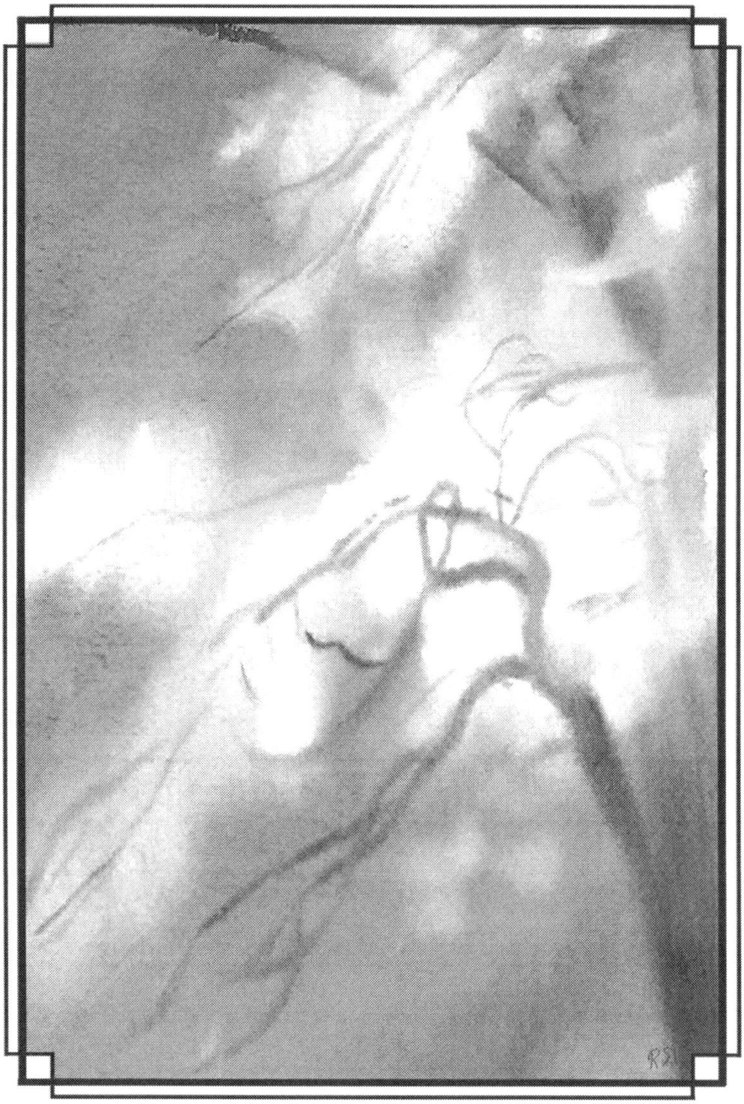

AUGUST

A Robin's Pledge

A robin lives for joy and romance,
He likes to sing and he loves to dance.
Make for him a garden, and he'll love you too,
Forever, it's true.
(If you give him half a chance.)

Now, if you thought July was busy, wait 'til you see August! Everything continues to grow so tall that it's about the nearest you can ever get to a jungle amid the once genteel British countryside, the land smothered by a thick, impenetrable tangle of greenery; weeds, bracken and ferns covering every inch of ground; columbine winding round the trees and bushes – everything eager for sunlight and often collapsing under its own weight into so many rank and tangled heaps.

The formal gardens are no less exuberant: marigolds and lilies, geraniums and honeysuckle, and every exotic variety of clematis that cling to trellis and arbour. The tireless bees still drone among the scented English lavender, which even now, if left uncut, refuses to cease flowering – while above it all, the canopy of trees at its most dense, provides welcome shade and solace for humans and wild creatures alike: all those for whom the summer sun is sometimes just a little too fierce for comfort.

Sunrise and Sunset Times at the start of August

London	5.24 am	8.47 pm
York	5.17 am	9.02 pm
Edinburgh	5.16 am	9.20 pm

What Robins do in August

As mentioned briefly in the last chapter, the late summer period marks the beginning of the moult and that peculiar phase of the year in which robins might seem to just disappear. It might not happen immediately – since the juvenile robins of a late brood will still be in need of food and protection and we still have to forage for them. But eventually you will notice that your once-friendly, ubiquitous garden robin is nowhere to be seen. What's happening?

Well, don't worry. We don't actually go anywhere special or far away. But the moult is affecting us now in earnest, and we just prefer to lie low. You see, our feathers really do need to last a whole year before they are replaced with new ones. That's a long time to look after them, which is why we endeavour to care for them every day through the process of preening.

So what exactly is preening? Well, it's a meticulous maintenance routine in which we gather an oily, waxy substance from a special gland at the base of our tail (called the Uropygial Gland) and then trail it with our beaks through our feathers. This is often preceded by bathing – if water is to be had – or sometimes a flutter in the dust (a dust bath, as it's called). It all helps with the process of cleaning our plumage as we endeavour to realign the structure of our feathers for optimal performance and for optimal insulation and weather-proofing during the rainiest day or coldest of nights.

There comes a time, however, when even the most diligently serviced feathers will simply wear out. Sometimes, too, and more often than any self-respecting robin would care to admit, our feathers become damaged by the presence of parasites or else become a breeding ground for lice. So in a sense, it is a relief to be rid of them, even if a bit unsettling for us at the time.

Helping Robins through August

As you can probably gather from the above explanation, there really isn't much you can do for your robins at this time of the year. The weather is warm, and there is plenty to eat. So really, we're just fine, albeit struggling somewhat with the moult.

Just keep an eye out, please, for those juvenile robins of ours, who – in the event of a late brood – might still be hiding away in the undergrowth waiting to be fed. As requested during the previous month's notes, leave them well alone, please. They are probably getting along just fine, too.

What you can do, however, is keep those cats at bay!

We do understand that you love your cats, but at the very least consider keeping them inside as long as feasible during the daytime, or provide them with a collar and bell to warn us of their approach. It has been demonstrated that these simple measures can significantly reduce the number of robin fatalities, especially of the many baby robins who perish between the mischievous paws of cats and other predators during the summer months and beyond.

Robin's plant of the month – English Lavender

There is little in nature more outstanding and beautiful than a vibrant, fragrant bush of English lavender. Its slender, silvery leaves and purple flowers grace gardens throughout the summer. It is especially attractive to bees in July and August – so many at moments, and all making such a buzz and a stir in the sunshine, that you can sense it and hear it from quite a distance. Up close it can be more than a little intoxicating.

Historically, the lavender, coming from the warmer climes of southern Europe, has always been prized for its distinctive fragrance and medicinal properties, either when distilled as an oil, or when crushed and placed in bathing water for cleanliness. The word 'lavender' has its roots in the Latin term for 'washing' or 'bathing' *(lavare),* so it clearly once enjoyed a widespread use in this respect.

The Victorians were very fond of it, notably for its fragrance in home-made perfume. A few springs of fresh lavender, sewn into packages, would be placed into cupboards or chests of drawers to sweeten any unwelcome odours. However, to give another person lavender in a posy, was not so acceptable, as the flower itself was associated with caution and even with mistrust.

The leaves and flowers are still used today for bathing and also medicinal purposes. A little lavender rubbed onto the skin is said to help ease the sting of minor burns. A little sprig or two under your pillow at night will help you enjoy a sound sleep with pleasant dreams – though I should just add that busy robins have little need of anything to assist us in that respect.

From a robin's perspective, it's easy to conclude that a spectacular clump of bee-teeming lavender with its frenetic activity might not be entirely suitable and would be a plant we would avoid. But not so. Apart from the bees, all those other winged pollinators that are attracted to the plant, inevitably encourage spiders to build their webs nearby, or even deep down into the stems and leaves of the plant, which in turn attract small garden birds like me to feast on the spiders themselves. They can't grumble, can they! A spider will spend its life trying to trap and devour other creatures, often cruelly. So it's a robin's avowed mission, I reckon, to turn the tables on them once in a while.

Jobs not to be doing in the Garden during August

Don't keep making such a fuss! Yes, it's just dandy when all this moulting business is finished and we find ourselves with a spanking new plumage to display to the world, but just right now we look dreadful, and we just don't want to be seen or disturbed. It's like when you have a really bad hair day, or someone comes visiting unexpected while you're doing the housework in your old dungarees. You don't want to be bothered.

We can't fly all that well either at the moment, what with so many of our flight feathers missing, and therefore cannot escape quickly from predators. It feels dangerous and it's frightening. So don't try and seek us out, please, even if you have a nice handful of sultanas or mealworms. We really can't be bothered now with superfluous food. Noise and commotion are not at all welcome, either. So there!

Yes, I'm sorry if I sound a bit irritable this month, but it's not a great time to be a robin, what with the moult and all the nasty itchy things we get in our feathers. And, like I say, we really don't feel compelled to eat ourselves silly at this time of the year, either. So please stop putting food out for us! Birds have more than enough to eat in the wild now, and those fancy feeding stations or bird tables in summer are arguably more for the benefit and entertainment of those who like to watch birds than for the birds themselves.

Worse, putting out food in the warm weather can contribute to sickness among birds because the seeds and nuts that remain uneaten can rot or become mildewed. Diseases can spread through the increased number of birds visiting the spot – the chances being that some of these will be unwell already and contagious to healthy specimens. Common diseases that are spread via unclean bird tables include Salmonella, a bacterial infection leading to inflammation of a bird's intestines; trichomonosis, a parasitic infection which affects our digestive tract; and avian pox, a viral infection of the bird's skin.

Elaborate feeding stations can also make birds lazy. They don't need to stand up and fight for their territory when a plethora of easy food is always available. So they become unfit and lethargic. There is even the possibility of in-breeding taking place because the youngsters are not driven away to seek their own territory, as would normally be the case when there's healthy competition among family members.

And finally, the accumulation of droppings from birds can fester and smell in hot weather, attracting flies and other pests, which means that a responsible gardener like yourself will be obliged to work doubly hard to keep the table hygienic and sweet. Ideally, it should be cleaned with a little disinfectant solution at least once a week – a lot of work on your part, and all for something entirely unnecessary at this time of the year.

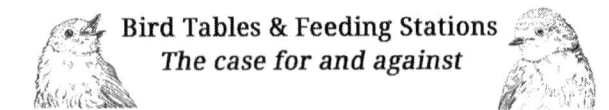

Bird Tables & Feeding Stations
The case for and against

Helps birds survive in harsh conditions, especially winter months.

Supplements nutrition at critical times such as during breeding or ahead of migration.

Helps with identification and understanding of bird species.

Educational for children and students - encouraging. conversation and ideas.

Entertaining for adults and the elderly.

Can attract aggressive bird species that squabble and fight.

Diseases among birds spread more easily.

Nearby nests more vulnerable to predatory birds.

Prone to untidiness and unpleasant appearance from copious bird droppings.

Encourages rodents.

Inbreeding possible due to lack of competition among birds.

More frequent window strikes from excitable birds.

The conclusion, on balance, has to be that feeding birds in the winter months is definitely helpful, but if you continue into the warm-weather seasons it is probably not. Far more important would be to direct your kindness into maintaining a fresh supply of clean water for us to drink and bathe in. Watching us birds enjoying your birdbath is every bit as entertaining as watching us eat. Moreover, this vital requirement for birds becomes, as you can imagine, even more crucial during these hot dry months of summer.

Naturally, this is also a time when your wildlife pond, if you have one, really comes into its own, providing a shallow area for birds to refresh themselves and drink – as well as other garden creatures, of course, such as voles or hedgehogs, those prickly little creatures with the pointy snout.

Robins love hedgehogs, by the way. Even though they are mostly nocturnal, our paths do sometimes cross in the evening or just after dawn. To us, they are like miniature gardeners. They waddle along and disturb the ground as they grub up food, and then we can follow and pick up all the dainty morsels they ignore or leave behind. We miss their presence in the winter because they hibernate – that is go to sleep for several months to ensure they get themselves through the worst of the cold weather.

It would be nice if robins could do that, but we can't.

Robin encounters a hedgehog at dawn.

The Night Sky in August

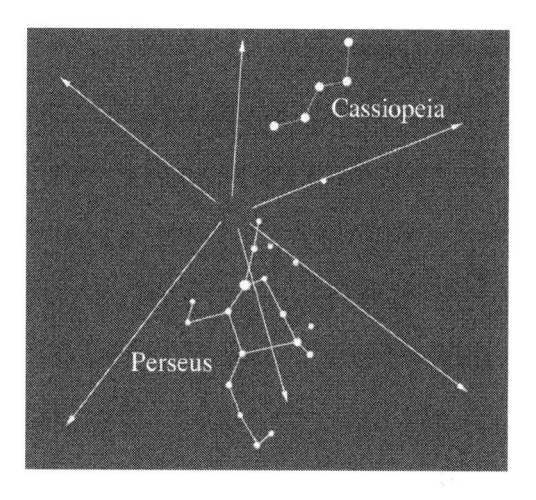

Do you enjoy watching shooting stars? Well, if the answer is yes, then mid-August is probably the best time to keep an eye on the night sky – because, usually just a little before the middle of the month, we are treated to what is called the annual Perseid meteor shower.

You should be able to observe lots of shooting stars at the peak of this display, and it's called the 'Perseids' because the meteors themselves (small particles of cosmic dust left over from a visiting comet long ago) appear to radiate outwards from the constellation of Perseus. The particles burn up as they encounter the earth's upper atmosphere, and despite having this common point of origin, they can be spotted just about anywhere in the sky, igniting spectacularly as they fall.

At this time of the year, Perseus can be found relatively high up, and probably the best way to locate him is via the nearby constellation of Cassiopeia, with its very distinctive 'W' formation of bright stars. See the diagram, and also the next chapter for more on the amazing story of Perseus himself.

If you have a hankering to watch the Perseids, do check your dates, because the peak of the shower varies slightly from year to year. And although some years are more prolific than others, you really would be unlucky not to see at least one shooting star if you stand outside for a minute or two.

The Milky Way and Summer Triangle mentioned in previous months' notes are still on view, by the way. So, as long as you don't have too much intrusive street lighting or a prominent Moon, it really is a great time to get to know the night sky and to find your way around. And it's currently not too chilly at night to be out there, either.

'Perhaps' and 'maybe' for Robins in August

In the way of all the seasonal occurrences in the robin world, the onset of the moult is not exactly a fixed and predictable event. It's usually well underway during August, sure, but it can definitely begin a little sooner depending on all kinds of variables.

The whole ordeal usually takes about six long weeks and also coincides roughly with our juvenile robins' transformation into proper, red-breasted adults. The lucky youngsters undergo only a partial moult during this, their first year, their wing and flight feathers still being relatively new and serviceable – so no need to be replaced. More of this in the next chapter because, again, it can be something you might notice early or late in the year according to when the fledglings vacated their nest.

Thankfully, for them and for us adults, too, not all of our feathers drop away at once. This is especially important for our wing feathers – so essential for proper flight. A staggered process evolves in which they will replace themselves in a precise sequence that ensures that we are never entirely unable to fly at any stage. Clever. But really, it's not much fun.

The good news is that by the onset of autumn, next month, the adult moult will certainly be nearing completion and you might also start to see the first signs of our own young red-breasted birds proudly strutting their stuff as they show off their new adult plumage, too.

Robin Wisdom for August

There's always a time
For old feathers to go,
A time to renew,
A time just to grow.

There's always a moment
To let go of fear,
To let go of doubting,
To listen, and to hear.

And always a moment
To wish yourself well.
And treasure the world,
Where you happen to dwell.

September

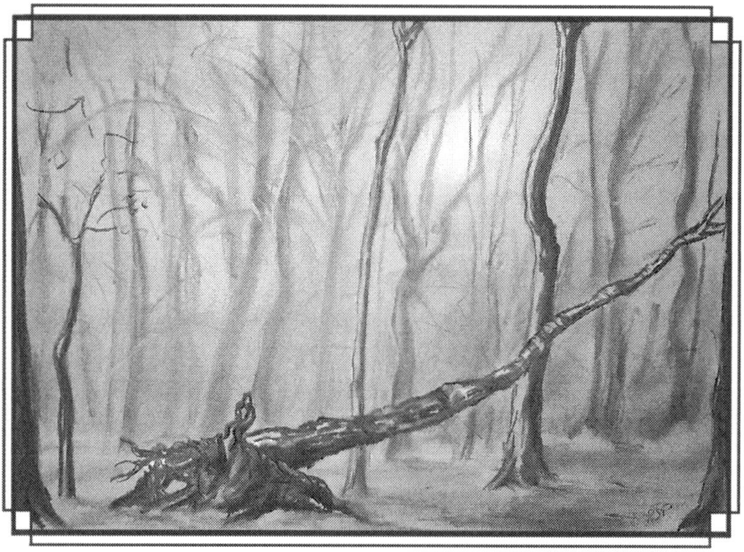

SEPTEMBER

Pride of Vest

What do you think of my new scarlet vest?
I reckon it's better than all of the rest.
It came just after my feathers fell out.
And now I'm ready to sing and to shout.

The rusty margins of the leaves and fronds of bracken that herald the autumn months begin to manifest in September, especially obvious towards the end of the month. Bucking the trend, however, and following a brief hiatus of colour in some of our gardens, are the pots, containers and borders, once again aglow with brilliant flourishes of fuchsias; dahlias; chrysanthemums; and dazzling pink nerines.

Despite the late 'Indian summers' that can sometimes last for many weeks at this time of the year, an obvious shortening of the days becomes evident, the evenings coming sooner and the nights hanging on a little longer. Warm, prevailing winds from the Southwest bring not merely showers but more prolonged spells of rain: a welcome change perhaps and a relief for parched gardens after a dry

August. The ground, now properly moist, brings a renewed vigour to lawns and flower beds, visited by hosts of butterflies and bees that, still unwilling to surrender to the ending of summer, continue to dance and flutter on their own secret missions to heaven knows where!

Sunrise and Sunset Times at the start of September

London	6.13 am	7.45 pm
York	6.12 am	7.55 pm
Edinburgh	6.16 am	8.07 pm

What Robins do in September

Sometimes, robins can still be in the midst of their moult by the onset of autumn's first month. But by the time of its conclusion, having finally traversed that difficult and challenging period, we can once again be seen in all our pomp, flaunting our spanking new coat of magnificent feathers and proclaiming our renewed self-confidence to the world with a little song by way of celebration. This will likely not be anything approaching the noisy crescendos of springtime heard earlier in the year, but now a little more doleful and melancholic, as befits the season.

The juveniles, meanwhile, perhaps lagging a little behind in transformation, are still well on the way to developing their red-breasted appearance. You will often see awkward, fidgety specimens in the garden that are half juvenile, half adult, exploring the world with all the curiosity and vigour of youth.

It's probably just as well that we robins cannot count, because, alas, many of their brothers and sisters will already have perished, picked off by predators. But those that you see, having made it thus far through the earliest and most dangerous phase of their lives will probably already have enough experience of the big bad world to survive and raise a robin family of their own soon, typically as early as next year.

Autumn is actually a very exciting season for robins, what with the winds stirring up all the fallen and decaying leaves. There's never a dull moment, because you never know what you're going to find by way of food lurking beneath. So if you get the suspicion that your local garden robin is somehow getting a bit larger in girth, you're probably not wrong. What with all those succulent fruits and berries ripening, it's just a huge feast from dawn to dusk.

The Robin Almanac

Windy days bring surprises.

Helping Robins through September

Continue to keep that birdbath topped up please, and, equally important, *clean*. I've just got my new coat of feathers, don't forget and, in the way of anyone with something fresh and pristine, I'd prefer to keep it looking smart, thank you very much. Bathing, remember, is also the all-important prelude to the routine of preening, and robins certainly don't want any dirty old water to be dipping into for that essential task. A slimy bottom and sides to the birdbath can also be dangerous if we slip and injure ourselves.

So how do you go about cleaning a birdbath? It's a serious business, I'll have you know, because it must be done safely without endangering any nearby plants or wildlife. Here's what you need by way of preparation ...

1) Eye goggles and gloves for your protection
2) An old scrubbing brush or washing-up brush (not one currently in use).
3) A bucket of warm, soapy water.
4) A jugful of cider vinegar or white wine vinegar
5) Plenty of clean, preferably running water for rinsing out afterwards.

Remove the bowl of your birdbath from its plinth (if it has one). Then, with a little soapy water scrub away any thick debris or encrustations with your brush. Pour this away safely, then mix up the cider vinegar with some fresh water and fill the birdbath fully. Continue working into any crevices with the brush, including around the brim. The ratio of water to cider vinegar is not so important, as long as you rinse the whole thing out thoroughly several times when finished. You can even leave the mixture to stand for a while if you like, in which case it would be best if you could remove the basin from where we usually expect to find it, so as not to risk birds jumping in.

When all is clean, rinse thoroughly. Do this several times, at a good distance from any garden plants or trees, until no possible trace of the water and vinegar mix remains. Always dispose of all waste liquids safely – preferably down the drain and not on the lawn! – before replacing the bowl back on the plinth and filling with fresh, clean water.

Wonderful! The importance of your birdbath really cannot be overstated. Keep it sweet for us and you'll have a grateful population of beautiful wild birds visiting your garden all through the year.

September

Robin's plant of the month – Asters

Asters, named after the Greek word for 'star' are common in UK gardens, and they are legion in the many recent cultivated varieties available in your garden centres. But the original ones, and those I like best, are called Michaelmas Daisies – another of those plants to take its name from an annual festival of the Church, namely the feast of St Michael or *Michaelmas*. Occurring on the 29th of September, Michaelmas coincides with the time when these beautiful purple-blue perennial flowers are at their best.

In Christian iconography, it was a time to commemorate the exploits of the mighty Archangel Michael who was said to have defeated the fallen Lucifer in an epic battle between good and evil. And the bright, daisy-like flowers of the aster were considered a perfect emblem to protect against the advancing gloom of winter when evil and wicked deeds were more likely to proliferate in the dark.

The *starry* name of 'Aster' meanwhile refers to the ancient Greek legend of the sky goddess, *Astraea* (the 'starry maid'). One day, the story goes, she looked down, and noticing that there were no stars at all shining upon the earth, became very sad. She wept and the aster flowers sprang from all those places where her tears fell. *Ah – isn't that lovely!*

The feast of St Michaelmas once marked another of those traditional 'quarter days' of the calendar when rural folk were paid for their labour, and rents became due. It was also an occasion on which one would slaughter and eat a goose, preferably one fattened on the remains of the harvest.

Now, as a robin, I don't know if I can condone the eating of birds, no matter who they are. But it was a practice that would not only ensure a bountiful supply of meat and fat but was also, oddly enough, thought to safeguard against financial hardship during the year ahead. Sounds reasonable … *I think.* And, after all, the goose is a pretty annoying creature anyway, isn't it? Honking away all the time and chasing robins.

As for the Victorians, well they were very smitten with aster flowers since they saw them as good for displaying indoors. But they did not award them with any particular symbolism or meaning other than as a celebration of friendship and, some say, of variety also. Variety – it's the spice of life. So, good old asters! Long may they thrive.

September

Jobs not to be doing in the Garden during September

Don't go trimming any shrubs or bushes that are already bearing fruit or berries, or even those that will bear them shortly. Not unless you really need to, for example if the plants themselves are diseased. Also, we robins are understanding creatures, and we realise that gardeners are sometimes a little obsessional about tidiness – all those straight lines and square corners that some of you prefer. It is tempting, isn't it, just to want to shape things up a bit? But don't be reckless, please. You might not be able to see the berries yet, because the bushes might only just have finished flowering, but they will come along soon.

For example, ivy, honeysuckle and berberis are just beginning to display their ample provision of berries now. And although we don't want to eat them just yet, because we don't need them anyway, and they are a bit on the tough side still, I can assure you they will be in demand later in the year. And not just for robins, but all manner of wildlife.

You could also try to stagger the clearing up operation – for instance, focusing on one section of the garden each year, so that some parts remain untouched – this being especially the case if you have a neglected or remote corner where leaving things alone really won't matter so much.

This sensible, one-bit-at-a-time approach to maintenance is really a good answer to that one perennial problem that lies at the heart of wildlife gardening – that is, how to reconcile the demands of wildlife with that of basic tidiness and orderliness. You want to be able to move around your garden safely, without too many hazards or nasty surprises, but obviously to do so you need to cut and shape things a little. There seems no 'good' time to be doing this. Cutting too early; trimming too late; digging in the wrong place; even sitting in the wrong place! There is always going to be some disadvantage to some wild creature or the other. Don't despair. Just pick on a certain designated zone each year. And then a different one the following year, and so on. That way you can manage your plot wildlife garden with sensitivity and without inflicting too much damage on your resident wild creatures and their ways.

And if you keep your paths tidy, everything else will fall into place, and look good, too.

The Night Sky in September

With the onset of autumn, you might begin to notice a large square-like formation of four stars becoming more and more prominent in the eastern and southern skies. This is the Square of Pegasus the Winged Horse of classical mythology. The square represents the top half of the horse's body rising from the sea, and as with so many of the constellations, it is not entirely easy to spot at first. But once you have succeeded you won't forget it. The main thing to remember when searching for it is that the horse is actually upside down, and the square itself is probably going to be much larger than you anticipate. It really does cover a substantial area of the sky.

The name 'Pegasus' means something like 'springs' in the way of water, and the mythical horse's origins are a bit grizzly. He is said to have sprung from the blood of the monstrous Medusa after she was beheaded by the hero Perseus. Thereafter, the winged horse made its way to Olympus and the abode of the gods, where he assisted Zeus in distributing the occasional thunderbolt.

Joined to the square is the constellation of Andromeda – yet another link in the Perseus legend since it was he, Perseus, who rescued the beautiful Andromeda from a horrible sea monster. See the notes for the night sky in October for more on this intriguing story.

If you know where to look, you can just detect a fuzzy patch of light to the northeast of the square, which is actually a great galaxy in the constellation of Andromeda – one of the most distant objects you can ever see with the naked eye. And it really *is* a long way off. The blistering speed of light, which travels at thousands of miles per second, is no big deal in relation to the vast distance of this object, so you are actually seeing it as it was two and a half million years ago. The light has taken all that while to reach you.

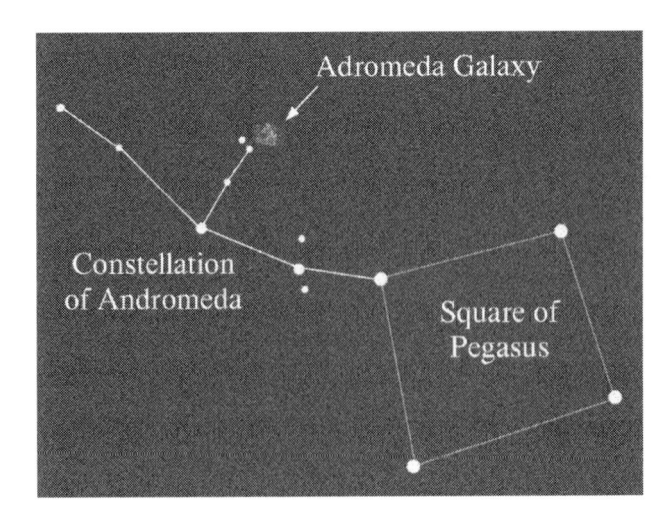

Adromeda Galaxy

Constellation of Andromeda

Square of Pegasus

'Perhaps' and 'maybe' for Robins in September

Sometimes the robin moult can begin later in the year than normal, so will obviously finish later, too. Don't be disappointed, therefore, if, even by the end of the month, robins have still not put in much of an appearance or you do not yet detect the renewal of our robin singing. Don't worry. Robins are irrepressible. Once the long moult is over, and we have our fine new plumage, we'll be back.

Meanwhile, towards the end of the month, some robins might already be considering whether to migrate and journey away from home, to fly to warmer climes for the worst of the approaching UK winter. Not all go, far from it. Some do, some don't; some succeed and return safely a few months later, some perish and come to grief. So, you see, for those who do choose to leave, it is one of the most perilous and courageous things any creature can ever attempt.

You just have to admire them.

To add to the mix, we also witness the arrival in autumn and winter of robin migrants from other parts of Europe or, sometimes, other parts of Britain. It's all change, and consequently, as the autumn marches on, there are likely to be alterations in the local robin territories and their boundaries, with absentees being replaced temporarily by robin visitors migrating in from elsewhere.

That's strange really, because I can't see that the UK is much of an attraction in the harsh depths of our Winter. Rather it just seems that, for some robins, 'change is as good as a rest'.

Robin Wisdom for September

Grim times,
When summer's joys are fled,
It can make a robin sad.
Bleak and darkling, full of dread,
But it need not be so bad.

For if you're sad or gloomy,
Here's what you can do.
Admit that there is sadness, yes.
But the sadness isn't you.

September

October

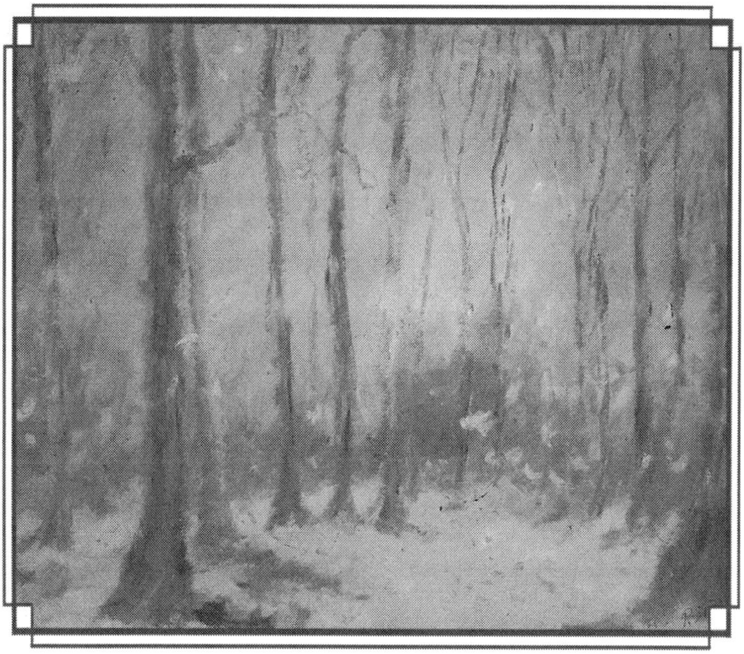

OCTOBER

Goth Robin

By ancient ruins, ivy clad,
Perched on bough in dusky gloom,
And neither joyful nor yet sad,
Sings robin redbreast at close of day.
Caught in the splendour of a bright crimson ray.

October really does usher in changes of major significance for robins. But it's a beautiful time. The woods and gardens blush and then positively blaze with yellow and golden leaves. The chestnut trees are usually first to turn, the oaks invariably last, while so many other once-verdant shrubs and ferns each according to its own nature and time will crispen and turn, as well. Aloof from it all, the latest gaudy flowers of the garden, the canna lilies, chrysanthemums, cosmos and clusters of pink and white cyclamen, continue to defy any suggestion of decorum, all plumped up with radiant colour.

Yet for all that, the season of change and nature's annual revolution when the old order is swept away is well and truly upon us now. And nothing, it seems, can ever elude it or truly be at rest. Darting across the skies, the swifts and swallows mingle and gather, readying themselves for their epic migratory journeys to the South and East. And in the woods, a moment when a solitary leaf flutters to the floor could be followed a minute later by a stirring breeze and then, before the day is out, a gale so strong as to bend an entire limb of a tree and scatter the brittle leaves in drifts everywhere. Then suddenly it is quiet again. A smoky fog and a silent mystery descends. A spell is cast with the darkness from which mushrooms and toadstools spring up overnight like magic to the puzzlement and wonder of all who chance upon them the next day.

It is all very unpredictable; very exciting – and robins just love it.

Sunrise and Sunset Times at the start of October

London	7.01 am	6.37 pm
York	7.05 am	6.41 pm
Edinburgh	7.15 am	6.48 pm

What Robins do in October

Birds are really in their element right now with the wind tearing through the gardens and woods. The change began in September, but now it comes on apace. We don't need to waste lots of energy grubbing about and throwing things aside, trying to unearth food. Nature is doing that for us, stirring up the debris wherever it might be, exposing numberless goodies for us to sample. The young robins cannot believe how much fun it is, exploring and learning, as every fresh gust of wind reveals yet more. Some of it is not so good to eat, of course, and is cast aside pretty quickly. It is 'school time' for robins, learning what can be consumed, and what should be left well alone.

This is also peak time for spiders – the spider mating season, they say. Well, you could have knocked me down with a feather when I heard that. I can't understand why anybody would fancy a spider, can you, even if you're another spider! But there you are; they say there's always someone for somebody – and even though the cobwebs are a bit of a nuisance, the smaller ones are very tasty.

As mentioned previously, autumn is also a period when some robins consider migrating to escape the worst of the winter. In the UK it is only a minority who do so, and most are actually female robins. At any rate, it's the chief subject of speculation in the garden at the moment – who's staying, who's going.

Invariably a migrating robin will journey alone. You won't find us all gathering together and setting forth in vast, ostentatious flocks as some species of migrant birds do – s*howing off.* Robins, ever the individualists of the bird world, single and brave, fly off alone, destination the south of France, Spain or Portugal. In many instances, those who go will set off at dusk and fly overnight. It's safer that way, and there are lots of navigational aids to assist, such as the stars, the Milky Way and the Moon. It's amazing to think of it: that solitary little bundle of energy on the wing, hurtling through the night sky above the sea, determined to make it across safely.

To tell you the truth, I've never felt the urge to go, myself. All those peculiar foreign places where the ground is so hard, you can hardly find a decent worm to eat. What's the attraction in that? Some robins just like the sun, I suppose. And then, a little later, all being well, the adventurous ones will return to their familiar stamping ground at the end of winter, reversing the long journey and often coming back to the exact same spot from which they began.

In doing so, they will have to weigh up the risks of returning too soon – that is, before the bad weather has properly dispersed, or else too late, by which time all the best territories and the best mates might already be spoken for. Decisions, decisions.

Helping Robins through October

Now is the perfect time to think about establishing nest boxes for next year's occupancy. Whether you purchase these from your local garden centre; buy online, or even build one yourself, the autumn months really are best for installing them. Next year's nesting season is a long way off, and it gives us robins ample time, therefore, to become used to the presence of the boxes.

Also, once located and secured safely into position, there is ample time for any foliage, like ivy or honeysuckle for example, to grow around and across them, providing vital cover and protective camouflage. For robins specifically, you should make sure the box is of the open-fronted variety, and that it is fixed at a height of around five feet above the ground. There are more tips and information about nest boxes and what robin's precise requirements are in my book 'The Magnificent British Garden

October

Robin.' In the meantime, if you really do fancy making one yourself, with all the pleasure and satisfaction that entails, here is a handy diagram showing how all the pieces you need can be cut from a single plank of wood.

6"	Lid 8"	Back 10"	Front 3" approx	Side 8"down to 7"	Side 8"down to 7"	Base 6"

3½ feet

Old, seasoned wood is always preferable in this respect and is best if untreated with preservative. All the pieces will be 6" in width ideally, or whatever width your single plank happens to be. The back of your box, when complete, will be a little higher than the front to take a slope for rainwater and, if required, a hole for fixing.

Handy tip: cut the base out last of all, because its size will be dictated by the thickness of your timber. Once assembled, the lid can be hinged with a little piece of felt or leather, so you can reach in to clean once the nesting period is over.

The completed nest box ready for deployment
(Yours *does* look like this, doesn't it?)

With the outdoor season drawing to a close, it is tempting, I know, to neglect the lawns and not to put the mower or strimmer to work as often as you once did in summer. But robins do actually quite prefer well-mown lawns. Yes, really! Some people will tell you this is just not true. They will insist that a proper wildlife garden doesn't have short grass. Well, I suppose there might be some logic to that assertion. Long growth does encourage the bugs and wrigglies, and I can't say I know of too many wild creatures who want to see stripes in perfectly manicured lawns. But robins are small birds. If we are fortunate enough to have the luxury of an open lawn in our garden, we do enjoy being able to hop around, to see things clearly and to give chase without interference.

Try an experiment, leave a bit of lawn to grow long and wild during the autumn, while keeping another area short. Then watch and see which side the robins and other birds prefer. Long grass is a waste of a good lawn, in my opinion. It gets in our eyes and hides the worms and crane flies from view. And there's plenty of wild undergrowth elsewhere, I'm sure, for all the bugs to enjoy.

So, now you know. No excuses. Get that mower out!

October

The first Endymion. Robin pondering the Moon.

Robin's plant of the month – the Spindle Tree

Although the spindle tree is plant of the month for October, the chances are that most of its beautiful pink and orange-coloured fruits that begin to appear sometimes as early as September, are probably all gone by now, especially if robins are about. Not for nothing is the plant nicknamed 'Robin's Bread' – we just love it.

The hardwood of the tree was once used to make spindles for spinning wool, and its toughness also lent itself to the construction of skewers, toothpicks and even – horror of horrors – bird cages. Preferring to grow in chalky soil or limestone areas, it is not that big as trees go, more like a shrub in fact, so it fits well into most garden settings. The small, greenish-white flowers appear from May to June and the autumnal fruits can't be mistaken for anything else, being an unusual colour of pink with a pretty orange-coloured seed peeping out from within. In size, the fruits are a bit like popcorn to look at. But don't eat them! They are OK for birds, but somewhat toxic to humans. Keep out of the reach of children.

Within the amazingly comprehensive Victorian language of flowers (hardly anything ever seemed to escape their attention), spindle blossom or seeds had the somewhat elaborate meaning of 'your image is engraved on my heart'.

So there you go: if you want robins to visit your garden, do plant a spindle tree. I can't promise that your image will be engraved in our hearts. But we will appreciate it greatly. And when it offers up its fruit in the autumn, you just won't be able to keep us off it!

Jobs not to be doing in the Garden during October

Continue, please, to keep in mind the advice from previous chapters regarding excessive or inappropriate use of chemical treatment for pests and diseases. Remember, you often have the choice of natural measures in this respect – especially the application of those nematodes mentioned earlier. These come in powder form and can be mixed with water and applied to the soil and lawns. Populations of helpful nematodes will build up in your environment over time and last for ages. So it works out less expensive in the long run, while also being safer for birds and wildlife. The subtle art of 'biological control' as it is termed, has been adopted more and more now in domestic gardening. A win-win situation for all concerned. But another useful concept is what is called 'companion planting.' This can be very successful in minimising certain pests, especially in an allotment setting or other areas where vegetables are grown. For example, it's helpful to grow some herbs, like sage or parsley near your carrots to discourage carrot fly, or to plant marigolds to ward off the whitefly that enjoy attacking your tomato plants. Lots of helpful combinations have been identified if you care to read up on them for yourself.

However, when all is said and done, a healthy, well-balanced garden environment will inevitably support healthy and happy plants. A varied population of birds, moreover, is also essential for controlling pests – caterpillars; aphids; snails and whatnot. In fact, there is scarcely any creature that fails to do some good in this respect. Even a pesky wasp will destroy aphids on the rose bushes, and even a slimy slug will clear up some of the debris and tidy up your pathways a little overnight.

In any case, don't be in such a hurry to sweep up all those fallen leaves. I know it looks a bit messy in places – but honestly, does it matter? Remember, we robins love to examine what's underneath the leaves as they settle in dank corners and along the edges of paths and beds. The variety of wrigglies that congregate beneath them as all the old leaves and seedheads rot away and decompose is amazing. It's 'party time' for robins during the 'fall' months of October and November, and we really would appreciate it, therefore, if you could refrain from too many bouts of obsessional tidiness at this time. As long as things are safe for you, and you aren't in danger of slipping and getting caught up in things, we prefer you to be slovenly for a little while longer. We are busy fattening up for the cold days, ahead. Don't spoil our fun!

The Night Sky in October

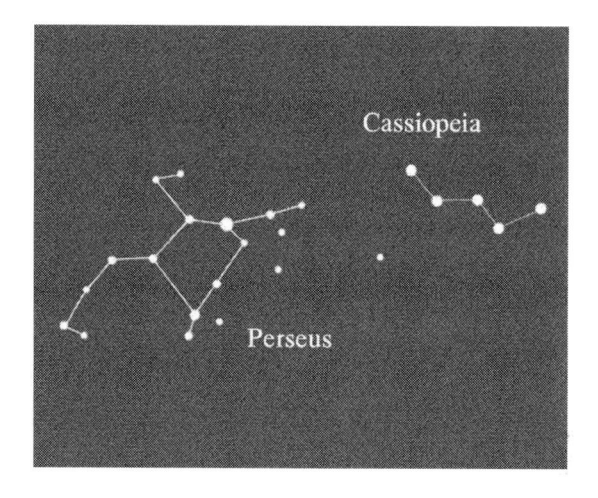

Another one of those constellations that are visible all year round in the UK is that of Cassiopeia, a beautiful compact collection of stars. You'll find it almost overhead in the night sky at this time of the year and is pretty easy to spot due to its apparent 'W' formation, also sometimes depicted as a lady seated, gazing at herself in a mirror. And, indeed, Cassiopeia, in mythology, was a bit on the vain side. She offended the mighty sea god, Poseidon (Neptune in the Roman pantheon), by proclaiming that she and her daughter Andromeda were more beautiful than any of the sea nymphs, the Nereids.

Bad move.

Poseidon was a bit put out by this, to say the least, and so he sent a sea monster to ravage the shores of the land. In horror at the devastation, Queen Cassiopeia consulted the oracle. She was advised that the only solution was to sacrifice Andromeda to the sea monster. Consequently, the young princess was chained to a rock by the shore to await her fate.

But the story does have a happy ending, because – as we saw in the previous chapter – the doughty hero Perseus came along in the nick of time; promptly slew the monster and took Andromeda to be his wife.

We must assume that Andromeda and Cassiopeia were gratified – it being a pretty persuasive reason to marry, I should imagine, when you've been chained to a rock by the sea and your suitor slays a horrid sea monster on your behalf. What girl could resist! And to commemorate such noble deeds, Perseus and Cassiopeia were placed together in the stars, the hero himself being located just a little to the east of his illustrious mother-in-law. The constellation of Andromeda, meanwhile, as we have seen, is not too far away, either, joined to the square of Pegasus.

'Perhaps' and 'maybe' for Robins in October

You will be aware by this stage, that a few reckless and impulsive robins elect to migrate in the autumn and to fly off overseas, their destination France or southern Europe. As to when exactly this occurs ... well, it could be now, or it might be next month. With robins, there are no hard and fast rules about exactly when and where. Each robin will decide for his or herself, and then once resolved there's no turning back.

Meanwhile, for those sensible robins that stay put – the great majority of us, in fact – the autumn months continue to provide a bounty of varied and delicious food. Really, you wouldn't catch me flying away from all this!

In other words, if you begin to notice that your local garden robin has suddenly appeared to put on weight, don't be too concerned. What with all the luscious maturing fruits and berries on the trees and bushes, it's understandable that many creatures in the wild will naturally put on a little extra body mass in preparation for the harsh winter months that lie ahead. It fact it is essential to do so.

That's my excuse, anyway.

Robin Wisdom for October

The time is nigh,
When a robin must decide,
Whether to flee,
Or else to abide.

Foreign climes will beckon us,
With promises galore,
But boldly facing winter's storms,
Is just as brave, I'm sure.

November

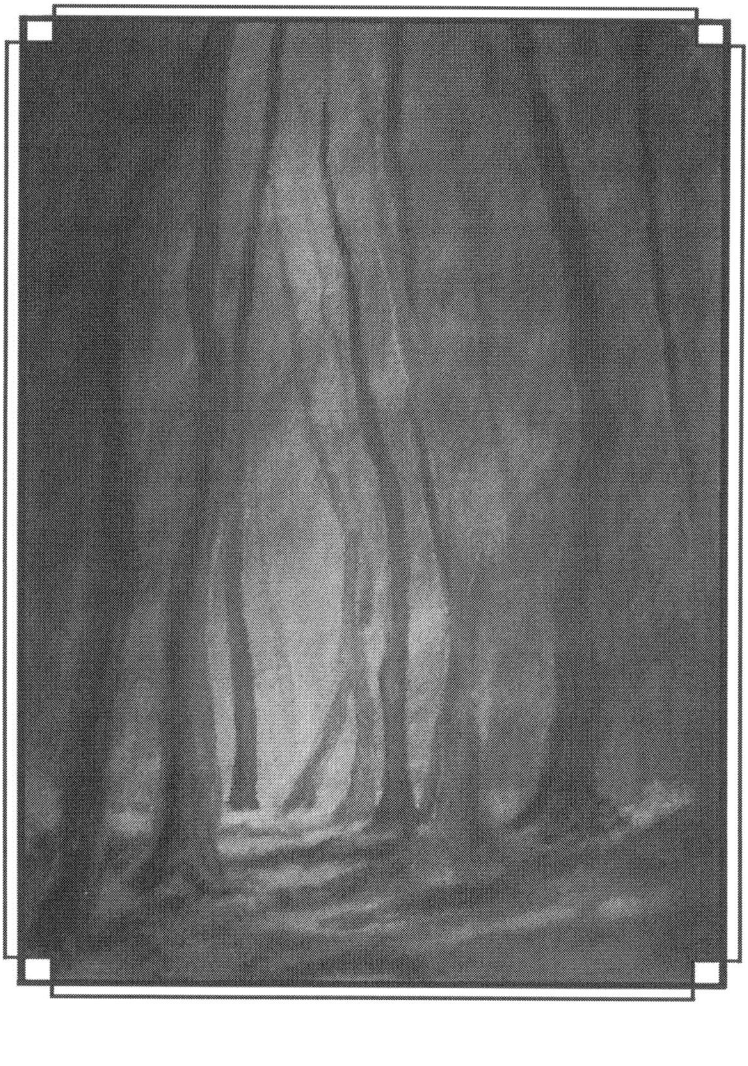

NOVEMBER

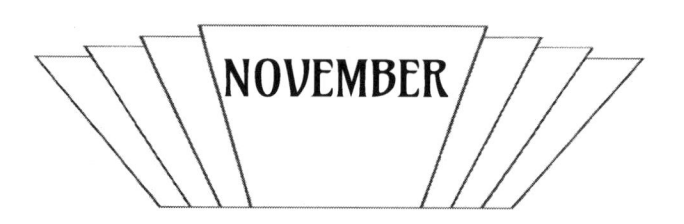

Comfort Eating

The robin I loved has flown away,
I hope she'll decide to come back some day.
Until that comes, I'll wait patiently,
And eat up all those berries on the old holly tree.

With the shortening days, the familiar trees - those that are deciduous, that is - are losing their leaves, and all bar the obstinate oak have become bare-branched and skeletal. Flowers whither in the garden, and succumb to the nip of harsh frosts and sometimes also of freezing rain and sleet.

But not everyone dislikes it. On the more passive days of November when the wind is scarce, there's a hush in the woods and gardens that is quite eerie in a *oldie,* Gothic kind of sense, and only we brave robins among the birds will venture a few melancholic notes. The mushrooms and toadstools continue to spring up everywhere, more so now than ever: a rich variety of shapes and sizes, each one decorative and beautiful in its own right.

Sometimes storms and even the occasional hurricane might sweep across the landscape, shaking the branches, breaking them and even bending the trees for a moment – while those living near coasts might dread the fierce waves and foaming tides that run with such relentless vigour towards them.

And yet, birds are amazing and full of surprises even now, for despite all the grim weather, on estuaries and salt marshes around our coast, the arrival of migrant geese and wading birds bring fresh and peculiar noises; harsh and insistent, their voices, echoing across the brackish waters.

Sunrise and Sunset Times at the start of November

London	6.54 am	4.32 pm
York	7.04 am	4.30 pm
Edinburgh	7.18 am	4.33 pm

What Robins do in November

Any robins that were contemplating migrating and leaving for a spell overseas, will usually be away now. They will be replaced to some extent by migrants flying in from Europe, arriving from places even colder than the UK – northern Germany, for instance, or Scandinavia. These temporary visitors are relatively shy robins compared to their UK cousins. They can be seen, *if they can be seen at all*, skulking around in bushes or the undergrowth, and not at all keen on mixing with people.

So don't be surprised if your friendly local robin suddenly appears to have gone all coy, resisting your advances with hand-held food and hiding away in the undergrowth instead. It's probably not your friendly local robin at all but a case of mistaken identity on your part: a European interloper. In the meantime, the one you thought it was is probably sunning herself in Portugal or the South of France. Don't worry, chances are she will return at winter's end, if not sooner, and will be seeking to regain her former territory, just as the continental robins here begin to depart.

Helping Robins through November

The nesting season for us robins is well and truly over now, so this is an ideal time for you to think about next year's campaign. You can safely clear out your existing nestboxes by removing any old bedding and then take time to clean carefully inside with a disinfectant wipe or a special solution of veterinary disinfectant. For your safety, please wear a protective mask and goggles to do this and dispose of old nesting material thoroughly. Also, take this opportunity to tidy up and trim away any surrounding foliage that might be surplus to requirements – all in readiness for a fresh family to take advantage of your bespoke 5-star nesting accommodation in the spring of next year.

As you go, you might find you need to replace a box that is no longer suitable or cannot be adequately cleaned. This is important. And after all, leaky or draughty nest boxes are a bit sub-standard, don't you think? Not at all suitable for us proud robins.

If you are buying a new box, therefore, or even making one yourself, do bear in mind that robins require open-fronted ones, not those with holes – which are for smaller birds like tits. Don't put this job off, please. Setting up a nest box now, securely in its place, provides us with a chance to become familiar with any new arrangement, so we will be more likely to make use of it when the time comes next year. You might also like to explore some novel ideas for a nesting shelter, like an old teapot concealed in a bush, or a logpile with a cavity for us to make use of – though in the latter case, make sure the pile is completely stable and will not roll about and squash the occupants inside.

By the end of this month, food will gradually become a little more scarce for us birds, so perhaps you would like to consider bringing back the bird table or re-establishing that bespoke robin feeding station from earlier in the year. But do please always bear in mind the precautions suggested in 'August' and the pros and cons of elaborate bird tables. Remember not to overdo it, or else your lovely, harmonious wildlife garden will become a chaotic free-for-all of crows, rats and any passing fox or badger – which will leave a terrible mess behind.

In this regard, a clever option and something you can easily make at home is a 'log feeder' – that is, a small log with holes or indentations drilled into it and into which you can leave scraps for us to enjoy. You can hang it above ground for our safety, and we will be on it like a flash. Otherwise, your local garden centre is usually a good place to discover plenty of other options, like bagfuls of ready-sorted nuts and seeds suitable for birds (no salt); or ready-made fat balls that can be hung from branches. See the earlier chapter of February for a recipe on how to make fat balls at home, because the same mixture can be plugged into the holes of the log. Remember, though, to avoid raisins and sultanas in the mix since these can be harmful to any pet dogs who might be sharing your garden.

Whatever you choose, do please try to place your offerings of food safely and discreetly, so robins can enjoy them in peace.

Log feeding station for robins (and other creatures)

Robin's plant of the month – Common Ivy

Ah, Ivy – or, to quote from a famous Victorian poem, *'How do I love thee? Let me count the ways.'*

Robins adore ivy. A garden without it is simply unacceptable. Coming into flower roundabout now, it features spheres of delicate white florets that will produce calorie-rich black berries. And although a robin would need to be pretty desperate to eat one (we really aren't that keen), many other birds love them. The nectar-rich, late-autumn flowers attract insects during lean times; and many of these little critters and their larvae will over-winter in the tangle of leaves and stems: a built-in larder for birds. Then there are the spiders – so many. It really can be 'spider central' in there sometimes, and we can take our pick of the smaller ones. In fact, it has been estimated that as many as 50 different species of wildlife are supported by this humble climbing plant.

Aside from being a fine place to forage for food, ivy is a plant robins are drawn to because it furnishes us with abundant nesting opportunities. The way the branches curl and twist into knots provides unlimited potential to build, and then the profuse, waxy leaves provide us with ample cover from prying eyes. Rarely does the rain penetrate into the depths of a mature ivy. And at night we can also find our way into the dark recesses of the plant to roost safely.

For people, however, ivy often gets a bad press because some mistakenly believe it damages trees and buildings by adhering and entwining itself around every branch and into every crevice. But those who really know about these things will tell you that the plant is actually independent, that it has its own root system (not parasitic in any sense), and that it actually helps to preserve old walls and buildings by supporting them and protecting them from exposure.

Ivy is evergreen, and so was sometimes gathered and brought indoors by folks in times past to provide them with cheer during the mid-winter gloom. The Victorians were very fond of it, as well, because it was the ultimate plant of the fashionable Gothic revival trend of the time. No self-respecting branch of the arts, painting or novel featuring old spooky buildings would be complete without ivy in there somewhere, dark and menacing, clinging to the ruins.

And of course, the strong, adhering nature of ivy was always going to find its way into the Victorian language of flowers – with attendant symbolism of devotion, matrimony and fidelity. Once the ivy holds on, it does not let go without being prised away forcefully: the perfect emblem of eternal love and eternal life. And so bridal bouquets would invariably contain a sprig of ivy, too.

Wonderful ivy. Train some against a wall, and let it grow and thicken. As long as it's not exposed to full sun (which is not good for nesting, anyway), it will thrive and become an enticement for birds all year long, including naturally your very own magnificent garden robins.

Jobs not to be doing in the Garden during November

Let's face it: gardeners love bonfires, and even non-gardeners love them in November – in part due to the enduring British tradition of Guy Fawkes or 'bonfire' night.'

Birds, however, tend not to share your enthusiasm. In fact, we hate fireworks. I've seen whole flocks of birds at night frightened half to death and even taking off from the protection of their roosting places in terror from the sudden flash-bang-wallop of fireworks. Poor things. They don't know it's a special occasion. They are not prepared. So it's a shock when it happens. Heaven knows where they finish up when they fly off in the darkness like that, and at what cost to their safety?

So please do consider whether your garden really needs to be an arena for this sort of thing. A proper wildlife garden certainly should never be. Public displays are numerous and certainly more convenient. Also, if you must light bonfires to get rid of garden debris instead of composting, please don't forget to examine the pile first for the presence of hibernating animals – our good friends, the hedgehogs for instance. Even though many parts of the UK don't have them these days, you really never know.

Which reminds, me, If you're lucky enough to have hedgehogs please do look after them. No, I don't mean taking them indoors as pets (they're not exactly cuddly are they?). But, as I say, they are becoming rare in some parts, so do watch out for their hibernation sites or even those places where they might be sleeping during the day. Check first before you thrust the fork in, or light that bonfire, otherwise you'll discover roasted hedgehogs when you clear up later, and you'll feel really bad about it.

Same goes for tending to the compost heap or bin (if you have one – see the chapter for March). There can be any number of wild creatures snuggling up at the bottom of the steaming pile, hibernating or keeping warm. Frogs, toads, slow worms, shrews and, of course, those hedgehogs again. Try to avoid disturbing the very bottom layer at this time. You can safely excavate that in the spring.

The Night Sky in November

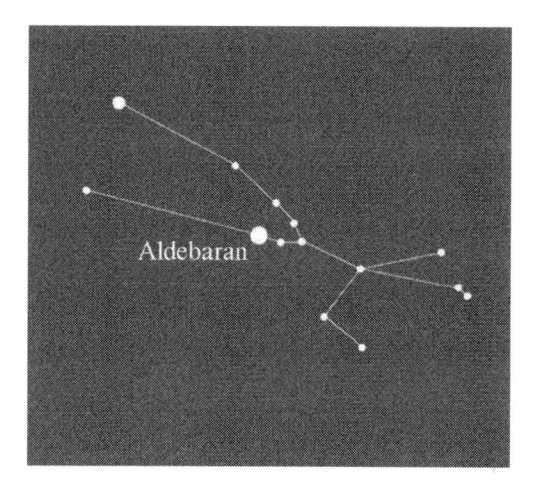

The autumn and winter months are good for spotting some of the more prominent constellations of the zodiac – that narrow band of sky along which the Sun, Moon and the wandering planets appear to travel. The Sun passes right through it during the course of one year, the Moon during the course of one lunar month. Taurus the Bull is a well-known zodiac constellation with a magnificent, Arabic-named star located in its midst: Aldebaran – bright red, and considered to be the angry eye of the bull itself.

The constellation is in honour of the chief of the Olympian gods, Zeus, who had a clever trick of visiting his prospective lovers disguised as all sorts of different exotic creatures to fulfil his amorous designs. For example, he visited Leda, queen of Sparta as a swan (honoured in the constellation of Cygnus) and he courted the lovely Europa of Crete as a Bull, which must have been a bit scary for her, I should think. But they seemed to have got on quite well together. Their child became the legendary King Midas – the chap who turned everything he touched to gold.

A modest meteor shower, the Taurids, occurs around this time of the year – so named because the shooting stars themselves appear to radiate outwards from Taurus, so check your dates and look out for those.

Nearby, meanwhile, you can find the zodiac constellation of Gemini, the Heavenly Twins – conspicuous due to two bright stars in close proximity, called Castor and Pollux. These are named after two mythological twins from, firstly, the legitimate union of Leda, Queen of Sparta with her husband, the King; and secondly the divine offspring of Queen Leda and the god Zeus (he of the swan disguise). So although they are called the Heavenly Twins, they are not proper twins, because Pollux, as the son of Zeus, was obviously immortal, while Castor was not.

The two lads grew up together as friends, however, and eventually became mighty warriors and horsemen. And when Castor was killed in battle, the grieving Pollux asked Zeus if his half-brother might be honoured by sharing in his immortality. Zeus agreed, and the two were consequently placed together in the sky where they remain in a constant embrace, together for all eternity.

November

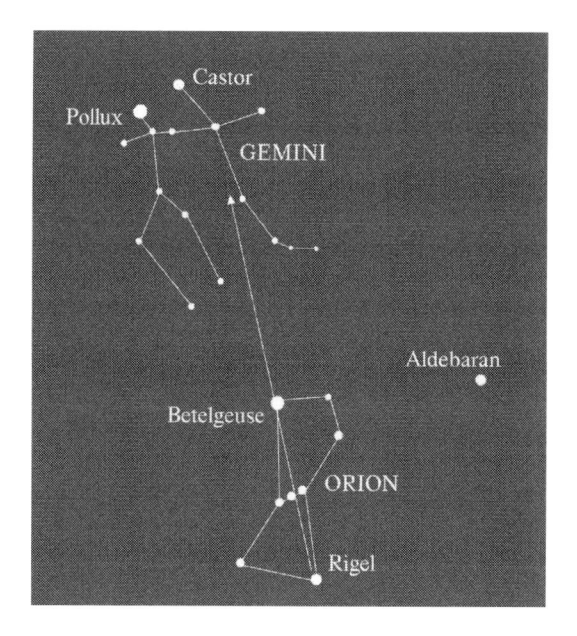

It's easy to find Gemini and its two illustrious twin stars. The constellation is very high in the sky on winter evenings in the UK, and you can use the stars of Orion in the south to make sure you have found it. Just trace an imaginary line through the two corner stars of Orion's body, from Rigel up through our old friend Betelgeuse, and it will take you almost directly to Castor.

'Perhaps' and 'maybe' for Robins in November

In some years, the month of November can still be unseasonably mild, especially at the start, and especially in the south of the UK. When this is the case, it is always possible that any robins that had a hankering for migration will have thought better of it and postponed the journey. A wide range of variations exists, dependent on the local climate; the availability of food or the likelihood of a severe winter in prospect. We birds like to think that we can instinctively predict these sorts of things and weigh up the advantages or otherwise of taking that bold step of flying away, but we can't, and we often change our minds.

With significant alterations in the local robin population, the ranges of individual territories tend to dissolve and alter at this time. This is accompanied (just for a short while) by an overall waning of enthusiasm for the process of defending the boundaries. And, as we have seen, those overseas robins are inclined to be a little more reserved in their ways. They are naturally shy and cautious compared to your bold and hearty British robins.

As many of our parental responsibilities are also on the wane now, this is a time when robins enjoy renewed freedom to once again come and go as we please. Free as a bird, I am! And though some relish the prospect more than others, of one thing you can be sure: that of all the qualities, treats and advantages a brave robin enjoys out here in the wild, liberty tastes the very best of all.

Robin Wisdom for November

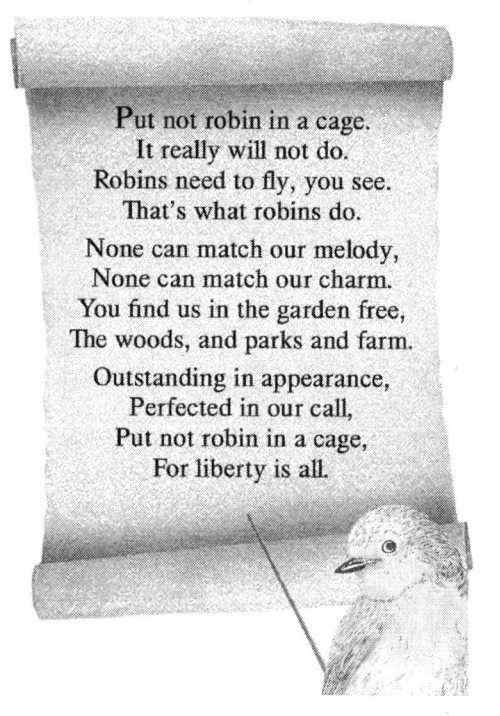

Put not robin in a cage.
It really will not do.
Robins need to fly, you see.
That's what robins do.

None can match our melody,
None can match our charm.
You find us in the garden free,
The woods, and parks and farm.

Outstanding in appearance,
Perfected in our call,
Put not robin in a cage,
For liberty is all.

December

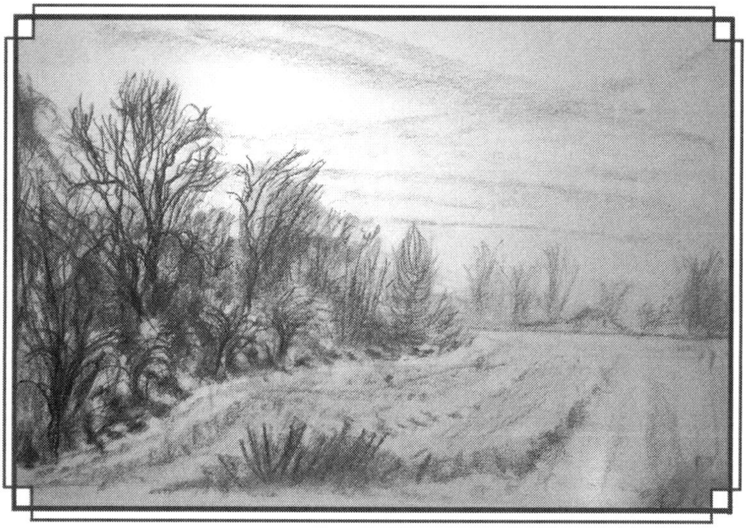

DECEMBER

Season's Greetings

At early morn, he greets you from the window sill,
A scratching and a tapping and a voice so shrill.
And not, just yet, with any certain reason,
Comes robin with a blessing,
For the joyful festive season.

The days are becoming very short once again as we approach the winter solstice (occurring just a few days before Christmas). And on some days, it seems that daylight has barely wiped the sleep from its eyes before it starts to dissolve again into twilight, and the typically dull, frosty skies of winter seem to have a hint of sunset in their colouring even at midday.

Apart from that, it can be a beautiful time of the year – especially if you take pleasure in all the varied shapes and structures of trees. There's no better time for observing them than now: the jagged and tangled oak branches that twist every which way, or the elegant arching forms of beach and hornbeam that always look so graceful no matter what the season. And then there's the birch trees, with their bright, variegated barks that peel away in patches – and all the magnificent dogwoods in the gardens, their stems all scarlet and gleaming in the low winter sun. What contrasts! It is all very lovely. Even we ever-more-hungry robins can appreciate that sort of thing, *if we have time.*

Sunrise and Sunset Times at the start of December

London	7.44 am	3.54 pm
York	7.59 am	3.46 pm
Edinburgh	8.18 am	3.44 pm

What Robins do in December

The short answer to the question about what robins do in December, or any of the winter months for that matter, is that we search for food and we eat. And we jolly well eat as much as we can. A robin needs to consume at least a quarter of its body weight each day to survive. During a cold spell, it is probably even more. Not only that, but our plight is cruelly emphasised now by an ever-diminishing timeframe in which to find enough food to see us through the increasingly long nights – as much as sixteen hours darkness in parts of the UK at this time of the year. On some days with the snow thick on the ground, it could prove impossible to find food anyway.

It is because of this potential absence of vital nourishment that we need to build up fat reserves in our body on a daily basis as a kind of insurance policy. Astonishingly, you might be surprised to learn, a robin can survive for a few days without eating very much at all if there's a bit of fat on the ribs to draw upon. But it would be a reckless bird who would rely on such a strategy from choice. It's impossible to know how long a really cold or snowy phase in the weather might last. So yes, we eat whenever we can, and as much as we can – which brings us nicely into the next section.

Helping Robins through December

As winter comes on apace, bear in mind that snow and heavy frosts put immense strain on birds and wildlife. Not only must we continue to compete for food, but we must also find places to bathe. Yes, even though it might be bitterly cold, we robins still like to dip into some water every now and again to preen our feathers properly – essential work if we are to fly well; escape from predators quickly and to remain warm and dry.

So, keep that birdbath ice-free, please, and without concealment from snow if you can.

In view of the importance of building up sufficient fat reserves on a daily basis, once again we really do appreciate that little bit extra now from people like yourself. As we have seen, birds in the UK can manage spring, summer and autumn perfectly adequately without assistance, and certainly without the provision of elaborate bird tables and endless supplies of nuts and seeds. But now in December, it's different. It's every bird for itself, and we really are glad of help during the worst of the chill, even if we must swallow our pride and tolerate all the aggression and pecking order of larger birds when food is laid out.

The deep mid-winter period is a time for reflection on so many levels, so it's probably not a bad idea now to consider conducting an audit of the wildlife garden. Is it living up to your expectations? The best way to start is by reviewing whether the garden has the following vital areas included. Firstly, does it have somewhere with an open, sunny aspect? This might not always be possible, but often it can be created with a little responsible pruning or felling. Secondly, does it have the opposite to sun: that is, a shady, woodland setting? This attracts a whole different population of plants, invertebrates and other wildlife. Even if it's just a small patch beneath a tree or collection of bushes, like holly, it's better than nothing.

Thirdly, does it have a pond or water feature of some kind? A wildlife pond, no matter how modest in size, is the beating heart of any proper nature garden.

The early days of December are just great for starting on a wildlife pond or altering an existing one. The usual creatures that will be living and breeding in water are not out and about right now or will be hibernating. And robins love to see you outdoors and digging anyway. We'll gladly keep you company as you expose lots of nice worms and things for us to eat.

When designing your pond, do take time to consider all your options. Choose a position with a fair bit of sun, and not beneath any overhanging branches or trees. You can buy a plastic ready-made pond and excavate some land where it will drop in nicely, or you can dig out a space yourself and line it with a special water-tight fabric such as butyl. The latter option is probably best since you can then create a surrounding boggy region: a bonus regarding the range of species that can be supported.

A wildlife pond doesn't need to be all that deep, by the way. You won't be wanting to put fish into these waters because they will eat up everything else, and the really interesting creatures like newts and dragonflies really aren't all that bothered about depth anyway – as long as it is sufficient not to dry out in summer.

Fill it with water and put plenty of rocks and plants in – which you will be able to do in a few week's time with a visit to your garden centre to explore all the wonderful variety of water plants available. You should always include a few vital oxygenating plants in the mix, as well as ornamental ones. Some of these will thrive in shallow water, some in deeper levels, and some are happiest in boggy areas. The main thing to bear in mind is not to over-plant. A properly functioning wildlife pond needs plenty of open stretches of water to succeed.

If you have a large garden and want to furnish it with a more substantial pond, then you can add more exotic varieties such as pond lilies, tall irises – or even reeds. And if you would like your water to be moving in places, consider installing a solar-powered pump beneath the surface. Be creative. The possibilities are endless.

Here's a handy diagram to get you started. It indicates some suggested levels for a small garden pond of, say, around four or five feet in diameter (though it doesn't need to be circular).

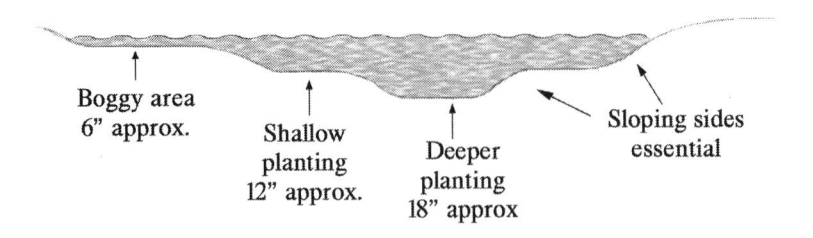

Boggy area 6" approx.
Shallow planting 12" approx.
Deeper planting 18" approx
Sloping sides essential

Whatever you do, make sure the sides are gently sloping so that birds and other creatures can enter and leave safely to drink or bathe. Birds can easily drown when trapped in deep water. And if you have children or pets, keep your pond safe for them, as well. Concealed fencing embedded in bushes can cordon off a pond pretty well, and a mesh of some kind just beneath the surface will always add an extra layer of protection. It's an interesting and fulfilling project for a boring winter's day or two when not a lot else is happening in your typical British garden. And come the spring you will be rewarded for your efforts and really glad you bothered.

Meanwhile, here's a guest list of those you can invite. Some of the creatures will come to breed, others just to drink. Or both.

December

Wildlife Pond Guest List

Frog and Toads
Newts
Slow worms
Dragonflies & Damselflies
Water snails & beetles
Pondskaters
Waterboatmen
Numerous insect larvae
Foxes & Badgers
Birds
Voles
Hedgehogs
Bees

Robin's plant of the month – Holly

If it's true that holly, with its prickly leaves and bright red berries, is one of the plants most recognisable even to the most indifferent of garden folk, then it is also definitely one of those most sought-after and beloved by robins. We appreciate the sharp, pointed foliage of a well-established holly bush or tree because it provides protection, and we really like the bright scarlet berries that, when ripe, are just the right size for a robin to swallow and get down in one go.

In pagan times, the winter solstice or shortest day was marked by what was called Yuletide. And long before the tradition of the Christmas tree was introduced into Britain, a substantial bunch of holly would be brought indoors and adorned with decorative items. It was a plant that (along with its associated evergreen of ivy), was bound up in numerous seasonal observances. It reminded the community that there was still life and vigour in the world, and that even in the depths of winter there was always the promise of brighter and more verdant days to come. Holly was also a fertility symbol, particularly a male fertility symbol, and so it also found it's way into various raucous pagan celebrations later in the year with the arrival of spring.

The Victorians cherished holly because, even as the vogue for installing a pine tree indoors at Christmas gained in popularity, the traditional evergreens remained steadfastly associated with ideas of eternal life. That is why we still construct our wreaths with holly and its red berries to hang on our front doors to welcome visitors. Meanwhile, for the Victorians, holly also indicated the quality of foresight. So, again, a looking-ahead to the new year.

By the way, if you're busy currently making a Christmas wreath for the front door, or even if you intend to buy one from the shops, do make sure it has plenty of natural components – that is, wreaths that have *real* berries in them, not those nasty plastic things. It's not that we robins would ever consider pillaging any of the berries, you understand. It's just that from a purely aesthetic point of view, one naturally prefers the presence of the genuine article.

Eat and be Merry for Christmas has come.

Jobs not to be doing in the Garden during December

Around this time of the year, with most of the plants dormant, many gardeners develop a hankering for labour-saving devices or solutions to 'permanently' control next year's weeds. They turn their sights on things like – horror of horrors – artificial grass or else soil membranes: opaque non-woven material such as polypropylene to place beneath the soil. It's a seductive proposition. The weeds just cannot grow through the covering, they say, and all you need to do is cut a little hole or two in the membrane wherever you want to pop your plants into the soil. Marvellous.

As an aspiring wildlife gardener, you really shouldn't fall for this. Yes, weeds won't grow through those swaths of hideous black plastic, it's true. Trouble is, the worms can't wriggle up through them either, so you deprive birds of a major source of nourishment. A year after laying it down you will discover new weeds germinating in the surface debris anyway – not to mention unsightly glimpses of black rubbery material rucking up and sticking out all over the place for people to trip up on. So, unless you really must, please don't bother with anything artificial that seals off the living earth. Good old tried-and-tested mulch is by far the best alternative for suppressing weeds. See the earlier chapter for March and for tips on how to make your own mulch.

Finally, do please remember, all jesting aside, that robins are moderately attracted to, and indeed often rely on many of your garden berries during winter, the holly especially, while many other birds enjoy the succulent fruits of ivy. They can provide nutrition during what is a particularly challenging period. If you go chopping all the best stuff away now for your

Christmas decorations, it's very upsetting for us birds.

Think about it: we've been patiently watching day after day as those lovely currants and berries mature and ripen. It's often very tempting to sample them, even when bitter, but we forbear knowing that they will be soft, sweet and delicious in just a few week's time. And then what happens? Someone comes along and pinches the lot for their decorations!

Leave some for us!

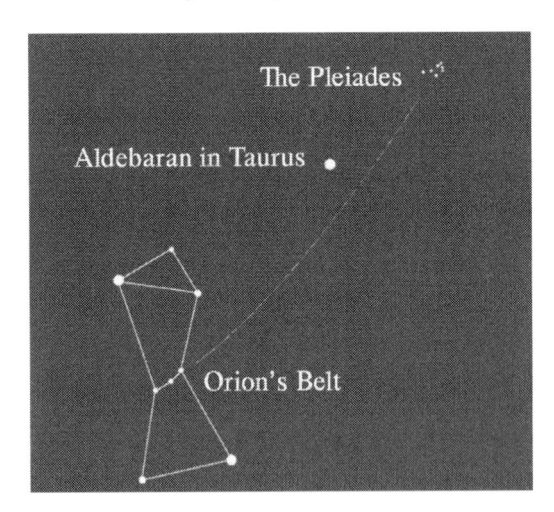

The Night Sky in December

Once you have successfully located the constellation of Taurus (see The Night Sky in November) and its bright reddish star Aldebaran, you won't have been able to ignore the presence of a magnificent compact star cluster nearby, and one, moreover, known and celebrated throughout history. It's called the Pleiades or Seven Sisters. On a good clear night, seven stars very close together can be detected with the naked eye, or so they say. In truth, most people can only discern six. Conversely, some really eagle-eyed stargazers will claim to see more than seven. How many can you see?

The name Seven Sisters in ancient mythology refers to the lovely daughters of the giant Atlas and his wife Pleione, herself the daughter of the sea god Oceanus. The story goes that the giant huntsman Orion (see stars for January) noticed them taking a stroll one day and, evidently in a bad mood, began to chase them – whereupon the mighty Zeus in a moment of compassion transfigured them into stars and placed them safely into the heavens.

Incidentally, you might notice another star cluster nearby in Taurus. This is called the Hyades. It's compiled of an obvious 'V' shape of loosely clustered stars, and although not as outstanding as the Seven Sisters, it does contribute to what is a fascinating region of the night sky.

'Perhaps' and 'maybe' for Robins in December

During the bleak days of mid-winter, a robin's thoughts turn to all kinds of grim fantasies. Remember, we have a life span of just two or three years on average – even though, as all mature robins well know, that so-called *average* is skewed considerably on the downside due to the many robins who perish during the first few days of life. As we have seen, a robin chick counts itself fortunate if it has survived the nesting phase of its young life. Many eggs are stolen or destroyed by predators, and it is common for nests to be raided once the little ones have hatched. So becoming a fledgling really is a great privilege.

Thereafter, it's a perpetual struggle to avoid all the horrid creatures out here that want to eat us. The truth is, not many robins make old bones or pass away peacefully in their sleep. And then there's always the weather to contend with, and who can predict that! Yet through it all, we still puff out our chests and we sing. We are brave little robins. And that is why, if you are ever anxious about things in your life, think on us, of how courageous we are in the face of dreadful adversity every day, and then you won't feel so bad. You'll be brave, too, and wonder what all the fuss was about.

List of Robin Predators
(They will eat our eggs, or even eat us!)

Buzzards	Sparrowhawks
Kestrals	Owls
Magpies	Jays
Crows	Squirrels
Foxes	Badgers
Stoats	Weasels
Snakes	Rats & mice
Seagulls	Cats

And even our beloved Hedgehogs sometimes.

Although wildlife in the UK won't usually experience much by way of snowfall until January – if at all, in the south – some years the weather really can buck the trend. There can sometimes be periods of snow arriving in early December. At the other end of the scale, sometimes the winter – especially the weeks leading up to Christmas when the autumnal winds have died down, can be surprisingly mild. I've even seen midges flying about in December, it can be so unseasonably warm – and so all a bit confusing at times.

One of the younger robins the other day even reckoned that winter was over because we happened to have a couple of sunny days. Said he couldn't understand what we were all so worried about and was just about to hurry off to find a mate and get started early when the weather changed. Freezing temperatures, howling wind and driving snow. That put a dampener on his fun and games.

Robin Wisdom for December

So many hate December,
It really gets them down.
It makes them glum and miserable,
And all they do is frown.
But when they say that life is pointless,
That's a funny kind of blindness.
For life is never pointless,
When you can show somebody kindness.

The Year's Renewing

So, now, at the close of the year, we have almost come full circle and arrived back to where we started. I hope this little book has demonstrated just how special your garden space can be, no matter how large, no matter how small. Whether it's the miracle of observing your very own local robin in May, becoming especially gallant and bringing gifts of food for his lady, or whether it's turning a corner in September and finding an unexpected clump of asters, the tears of Astraea who once wept because she saw so few stars upon the ground, you'll find that the garden is full of surprises, and full of enchantment ... if you allow it to happen.

I like Christmas, not least because just for a few short days everyone makes an effort to be nice to one another, a wonderful demonstration of kindness and courtesy. Placed as it is at the heart of the social calendar – some maintain at the very heart of everything we value and cherish – it's a few good days worthy of celebration. And what with us robins always so much a part of it, perched there looking out at you with cheery optimism on your cards, wrapping paper and decorations, life can feel, for a short while, warm and comforting and safe.

Did you know that robins are called *robins* because of Christmas? We used to be called *redbreasts* once upon a time, and going back even further, to medieval times we were even called something entirely different – namely, ruddocks. A trend occurred in Tudor and Elizabethan times, to add Christian names before those of birds – so the humble wren became the jenny wren, and the redbreast became robin redbreast, and so on. But during the early Victorian period, when the exchange of greetings cards at Christmas became fashionable, and when the postmen wore bright red tunics and were nicknamed 'robins,' we lost the *redbreast* part of our name entirely, becoming simply robins, too – and thus forever associated with the joyous festive season.

So, is Christmas, as some maintain, just another version of the much older celebration of the Winter Solstice? No, that's not entirely accurate. According to our modern calendar, the shortest day falls a few days before Christmas, not upon it. So, in addition to celebrating the birth of that one very special infant long ago, it seems that Christmas is not really about marking the closing of the year at all but rather the prospect of the next. That's an exciting proposition, isn't it? Perhaps nothing really ever ends, anyway, even the short life of a robin. Perhaps it's just the beginning of a fresh cycle, like the start of a new day, an opportunity to spread our wings once more and fly to deeds anew.

GLOSSARY

Brood – a term for the number of young birds successfully hatched within a nest.

Brooding – the spreading of wings gently over the eggs or the nestlings to protect them and to keep them warm and dry, particularly during the days after hatching.

Brood patch – an area on the abdomen of a female robin void of feathers and which, during the nesting season, enables her warmth to conduct more effectively onto the surface of the eggs. The patch disappears and is replaced by regular plumage after nesting is over.

Cloaca *(Plural = cloacae)* – a term that refers to the internal cavity from which the urinary and intestinal organs of birds have their opening, and within which the sexual organs are also operative. Copulation occurs when the cloacae of the male and female robins come briefly into contact.

Clutch – the total number of eggs in the nest. Typically between 4 and 6 eggs for a UK robin.

Commensal feeding – a term applied when birds supplement their diets by following other creatures about, like gardeners, who stir up invertebrates and other prey as they go about their work.

Constellation – a distinct grouping of stars that bear the name of a mythological being or creature from the past, typically from the ancient Hellenic civilisations where many of the original constellations were identified and compiled. Astronomers still like to refer to them, as it helps to divide up the night sky conveniently.

Copulation – the act of sexual intercourse between creatures. This only occurs during a few months in the year for robins, but it can be a daily occurrence once a nest has been built and eggs need to be fertilised.

Deciduous – applied to trees or bushes that shed their leaves in the autumn, and grow them back again in the spring.

Dehydration – the condition whereby an organism becomes stressed after losing more fluid than it takes in. Adequate levels of water are essential for many vital biological functions. Thirst is warning a sign of becoming dehydrated.

Equinox – two days of the year, in spring and autumn, with equal periods of daylight and darkness, or days and nights of equal length.

Erithacus the scientific name for the robin species. The British Robin is of the sub-species Erithacus Rubecula.

Fledge – a verb describing the process during which a young bird gains its full complement of feathers, enabling it to leave the nest and fly.

Glossary

Fledgling – a young robin who has vacated its nest and flown for the first time. It is only applied to robins for the first few days after leaving the nest. Thereafter, the term 'juvenile' is used.

Hatchling – the very young robin just after it has hatched – that is, having broken through the shell of its egg and emerged.

Incubation – the process by which the female robin sits on her clutch of eggs, thereby conveying her body heat to them. The warmth encourages the embryo inside to grow and eventually to hatch from its shell.

Invertebrates – creatures who do not have a backbone or skeletal system. Insects and spiders are invertebrates and robins are very fond of them.

Juvenile – describes a young robin, a stage usually reached a few days after leaving the nest. The term continues to be applied right up until the time of its partial moult in late summer when its adult redbreast feathers finally emerge.

Language of Flowers – A canon of symbolic associations between flowers and human emotions and experiences that, in a social setting, serves as a means of subtle communication. Its origins go back to at least Tudor times, but it flourished and reached a high level of sophistication during the Victorian era.

Migration – for robins, the process of travelling long distances during the winter to more supportive environments, usually overseas. The journey is reversed a few months later in time for the new breeding season back home.

Nestling – a popular term applied to a young robin developing and growing its feathers within the confines of the nest.

Moult – the annual loss of feathers followed by their replacement with new ones. For adult robins this takes place during the late summer period, after nesting and rearing of the young is over. It can take several weeks.

Mulching – the process of applying well rotted compost or leaf mould to the soil. Blocking light from the earth helps to prevent weeds from germinating, while also providing an environment in which invertebrates thrive.

Planets – the planets are our nearest neighbours in space. They orbit the Sun, as does the Earth. Unlike the fixed stars, however, which are very distant, they appear to alter their positions, night to night, over any given period. Their brightness alters, too.

Predation – the act of one creature preying upon another. Attacking or plundering something living – such as vulnerable birds or chicks in a nest.

Preening – the process of maintaining and aligning feathers with the beak, and during which a special oil from the uropygial gland is trailed through the plumage.

Roost – the place where birds go at night to sleep. Roosting or 'going to roost' is the act of finding a suitable sleeping place.

Solstice – two days of the year, in summer and winter, when the longest day occurs (summer), or shortest day (winter).

Glossary

Uropygial Gland – the small gland situated on a robin's lower back near the base of its tail and from which an oily substance can be extracted to assist in the process of preening. The oil also acts as a water repellent, thus keeping the flesh beneath the feathers dry.

Zodiac – a narrow band in the sky along which the planets, the Sun and the Moon appear to travel. Twelve constellations make up the background of the zodiac, and the Sun will pass through all of these during the course of the year.

Significant Dates on the Calendar

January 1st. New Year's Day

January 6th Epiphany Eve or Twelfth Night

February 2nd Candlemas Day.

February 14th St. Valentine's Day.

March 1st St David's Day, Patron Saint of Wales, and the first day of meteorological spring.

March 17th St. Patrick's Day, Patron Saint of Ireland.

March 21st Spring Equinox and the ancient pagan festival of Ostara.

April 23rd St. George's Day, Patron Saint of England.

June 1st. First day of meteorological summer.

June 21st The summer solstice, and the pagan festival of Litha.

September 1st. The first day of meteorological autumn.

September 21st. The autumnal equinox and the ancient pagan festival of Mabon.

September 29th. Michaelmas Day.

October 31st. All Hallows' Eve followed by All Saints' Day.

November 5th Guy Fawkes' Night.

November 11th. Martinmas and Armistice Day.

November 30th. St Andrew's Day, Patron Saint of Scotland.

December 1st. The first day of meteorological winter.

December 21st The winter solstice and the ancient pagan festival of Yule.

December 25th Christmas Day.

INDEX

A

Alarm calls 87
Aldebaran 187, 206
Attraction 45-46
Altair 105
Andromeda 154, 171-2
Arcturus 88-89
Assertiveness, stages 31
Asters 149-150
Astraea 150

B

Bathing 129, 99-100
Berries 19, 33, 100, 151, 183, 202-06
Biological control 169
Birdbath 33, 99, 116, 135, 147-148
Bird tables 13, 132-34, 180
Blackthorn 85-86
Bluebells 66-67
Boötes 88-89
Breeding season 71
Brood patch 62, 79, 213
Buzzard 81

C

Canis Major 37
Castor & Pollux 188-89
Caterpillars 71, 80, 85
Cats 68, 86, 130
Cassiopeia 137, 171-72
Christmas 195, 202-03 210-11
Cloaca 61-62, 213
Clutch 61, 213
Compost 48-49, 186
Companion planting 169
Continental robins 179
Courtship rituals 22, 46, 61

D

Daffodils 28, 35
Death 68

Deneb 105
Disease 129, 99, 133

E

Eglantine rose 101-2
Eggs 60-62, 79, 83, 121

European robins 179

F

Faecal sac 80
Fat ball recipe 34
Feathers 87, 113, 128-29, 138-9
Feeding stations 12-13, 83, 132-4, 197
Feeding young 71-72, 80-81, 83, 90, 97, 113

Fighting 30-31
Fleas 114
Fledgling 71-72, 86, 97, 103, 215
Food 10-11, 14, 132-3, 163,
Frogs & Toads 36, 96 186

G

Garden chemicals 49, 102-3
Garden tidiness 151-152, 170

Gemini 188-89
Great Bear 53-4, 89

H

Habitat 2-3
Hatchling 79-80, 215
Hawthorn 71, 84-6
Hedgehogs 135-36,

Hercules 70
Holly 202-3, 205
Honeysuckle 117-18, 151, 164

I

Incubation 61-2, 79, 121, 215

Ivy 48, 151, 183-5, 202, 205

J

Juvenile 113, 128-9 138, 144-5, 215

Index

K
Kestrel 81, 111

L
Lavender 118, 130-31
Leo 69-70
Lice 99, 114
Life expectancy 68, 208
Logpile 180
Log feeder 181-2

M
Magpies 33, 83, 96
Mating 22, 60-61
Mealworms 13, 33, 83
Meteors 137-8, 188
Michaelmas daisy 149-150
Migration 155, 163, 172, 190, 215
Milky Way 120-121, 138
Moult 113, 216
Mousetraps 119
Mulching 49, 205, 216

N
Naming 210-11
Nematodes 102, 169
Nemean Lion 70
Nest box 52, 164-5, 179-80
Nest box cleaning 179-180
Nest construction 45, 60-61, 65
Nest Hygiene 80, 179-180
Nest location 81, 164
Nest occupancy 72, 79-81
Newts 36, 51, 199

O
Orion 20-22, 37, 189, 207

P

Pairing up 29-30, 45-6
Pegasus 153-54
Perseus 137-38, 154, 172
Perseids shower 137-138
Plumage 33, 114, 129, 139
Pole Star 53-4
Predators 207-8, 216

Pleiades 206-7
Plough, the 53-4, 89
Pointers, the 53-4
Pond, wildlife 36, 198-201
Preening 128-9, 147, 216
Primrose 50-51
Protection of nests 33, 106

R

Red breast, forming 103, 144
Redbreast, name 210-211
Robin's Bread 168

Rodents 83, 96
Roosting 85, 101, 184, 216
Ruddock 210

S

Seven Sisters 206-7
Sex differentiation 62
Sheds 14
Shooting stars 137-8, 188
Singing 11, 29, 30, 95
Sirius 37-8
Slow worms 36, 186

Snowdrops 17-18
Song 28, 95, 111

Spiders 118, 131, 163, 183
Spindle tree 168-9
Squirrels 33, 83
Summer Triangle 104-105, 120, 138

T

Taming 48
Taurus 187-8

Territory 3, 11-12, 29, 45, 133, 190

U

Uropygial gland 129, 217

Ursa Major 53

Index

V

Victorian art 184
Victorian era 203, 215

Victorian flower symbolism 184, 203, 215
Vega 105, 120

W

Wild Garlic 66-7
Wings 61, 139

Wild rose 101-02
Worms 14, 29, 80, 96, 102, 205

Y

Young robins 80, 103, 163

Yuletide 202

And finally

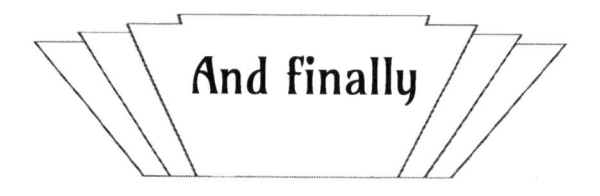

Other books by A. Robin, Esq.

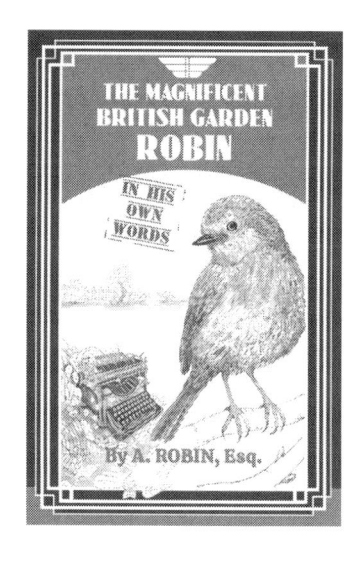

Available in paperback, hardcover and eBook. A splendid gift, especially at Christmas.

And if you're on the internet, why not hop over to my website: www.the-british-robin.com

Toodle-Pip!